Award-Winr

Jack L. Hayes

"Say it ain't so, Joe!"

Two Centuries of
Deception, Cheating, Gambling & Doping
in America's National Game

Books by Jack L. Hayes

Award-Winning Baseball Author
Jack L. Hayes

"Say it ain't so, Joe!"

Two Centuries of
Deception, Cheating, Gambling & Doping
in America's National Game

GoMyStory.com
3070 Collins Court
The Villages, FL 32163
757-439-7700
John@GoMyStory.com
www.GoMyStory.com

Edited by Kim Prince
Content Editors: Kim Prince, John W Prince

Cover design: John W Prince/GoMyStory.com
Photo Credits/Front Cover: baseball glove and background (iStockphoto/Image Source); money (iStockphoto/design 56)
Photo Credit/Back Cover: iStockphoto/jaflippo

Page Design: John W Prince/GoMyStory.com
Typography / Body type: Iowan Old Style

First edition 2019. Printed in the United States of America

Jack L. Hayes

"Say it ain't so, Joe!" Two Centuries of Deception, Cheating, Gambling & Doping in America's National Game

Award-winning baseball author Jack L. Hayes lays out facts to prove that the history of America's National Pastime is riddled with mistakes, half-truths, and outright lies. And it's all part of what makes baseball America's national game.

ISBN: 978-0-9911776-5-3

GoMyStory.com

To DARLENE —

Certainly not because I think that I should,

but because *I want to!*

Contents

Acknowledgments

This book could not have been written without help. I am indebted to so many people who, in one way or another, contributed their knowledge and assistance. As baseball fans everywhere know, the tipping of the cap is an acknowledgement of recognition, honor, respect, and gratitude.

Therefore, tipping of my cap and many thanks goes to the authors of such books as *The Book of American Pastimes* (1866), *The National Pastime, a history of baseball* (1910), *Eight Men Out* (1963), *The Fix is In* (1995), *Juiced* (2005), *Burying the Black Sox* (2006), *Steroid Nation* (2007), *Bases Loaded* (2009), *Alexander Cartwright: The Life Behind the Baseball Legend* (2009), *Baseball in the Garden of Eden: The Secret History of the Early Game* (2011), *Pete Rose: An American Dilemma* (2014), plus insightful reports by ABC and ESPN networks, and articles by *Sports Illustrated* and other magazines.

Also, helping to minimize my research workload were the contributions of articles by members of the Society of American Baseball Research (SABR), and John Thorn, the official historian of Major League Baseball. They made my quest to discover the truth, as defined throughout this book, much easier.

A special thanks to my good friend, Enrico Albanesi, for his help and never-ending encouragement.

I am also very appreciative of John Prince, and his team at GoMyStory.com, for bringing this project to fruition.

– Jack L. Hayes

Preface

Don't read this book, if you don't want to learn about the history of a sport filled with deception, cheating, and lies. Or want to continue believing in the mythical world of Major League Baseball, as it has been portrayed for over two centuries.

Last year, my award-winning book, *Baseball's Greatest Hits & Misses,* was published. It is filled with a variety of truthful, interesting, and inspiring stories about a number of legendary happenings that took place on and off big league fields. Yes, baseball's history is rich with interesting characters and stories. This game is not just a sport. It holds a special place in American culture.

Even our language is sprinkled with baseball jargon—it's in the ballpark (reasonable bounds); home run (to excel); strike out (fail); way off base (confused); batting a thousand (getting everything correct); big hitter (top person in his/her field); closer (person brought in to close a deal); curve ball (an unexpected surprise, and usually unpleasant); hit a grand slam (major accomplishment); and one base at a time (a step-by-step approach). These examples show how ingrained America's National Pastime is in our culture.

Baseball transcends different eras. It is filled with many things that make up its triumph and glory—Lou Gehrig's heart-breaking, "Luckiest man alive" speech (July 4, 1939); Jackie Robinson breaking the color barrier (1947); Hank Aaron (1974) breaking Babe Ruth's career home run record (and, in stark contrast, Barry Bonds' pursuit of Aaron's 755 homers thirty-three years later); Bobby Thomson's "Shot Heard 'Round the World" homer (1951); Mazeroski's home run to win the 1960 World Series. And, who can forget those Yogism's? This one in particular: "It ain't over until it's over." And nothing fits this saying better than the Cleveland Indians overcoming a twelve run deficit to defeat the Seattle Mariners 15–14, in eleven innings (August 5, 2011).

Behind all the triumph and tragedy, the winning and losing, the game also has a dark side. And, this is what this book is about. From the very beginning of structured baseball in America, a loosely-organized movement was underway to hijack the history of the game. Men like Albert Spalding and Henry Chadwick, along with the calculating exponents of Abner Doubleday and Alexander Cartwright, were not simply manipulators and liars. They were determined architects, hell-bent on doing whatever was necessary to control and shape the history of baseball. This book includes tales about all of this conniving, including the "black eye" that I gave to the National Baseball Hall of Fame (NBHOF) for allowing an undeserving player's plaque to remain mounted in the Hall... even after those in charge of the NBHOF received evidence that it shouldn't be there. Chapters 1–3 have all of the facts.

Chapter's 4 and 5 focus on gambling and game fixing. By its very nature, gambling on baseball is a risky business. In placing a bet, a gambler is either betting on a hunch, or expert knowledge, on which team will win in this highly unpredictable sport. But when the *fix is in*, the gambler has a "sure thing;" a guaranteed win. Here you will also find the highlights of U.S. Supreme Court (May 14, 2018) ruling legalizing betting on baseball, football, basketball, and other sports in most states; and its potential impact. I am a believer in that old saying, "The past is the best predictor of the future." With that said, I have provided a few examples to show just how destructive gambling, and game fixing, can be.

In the meantime, it was discovered that many players knew gamblers were bribing teammates, the owners also knew it was going on, and most importantly, the players knew that the owners knew—and they also knew that no action was being taken by the owners, out of fear that a scandal would damage organized baseball.

Well, that is just what happened! Chapter 5 is about *The 1919 Big Fix: 100 Years Later.* Much has been written about this historymaking fix in *Eight Men Out* (1963), and bevy of other books and articles. It was also portrayed in the 1988 movie, *Eight Men Out.*

But, hang on; I do not intend to bore with a rehash of what you already know. However, keep in mind that this chapter is being written 100 years after the events of *the big fix*. And, while the basic tale remains the same, you will be privy to reading about some newly discovered facts that were uncovered forty-three years later, hidden in the basement of Comiskey Park. In addition, another collection of "missing" documents was found in 2013. These two finds caused researchers, and sports experts, to take a fresh look at the accuracy of what had been written decades ago.

Research is a powerful tool. And, during my probing, I came across a few recently discovered documents that went beyond the scope of the 1921 "Black Sox Trial." This seldom reported trial related to the conflict ridden 1924 civil lawsuit jury trial, held in Milwaukee, Wisconsin. It pitted "Shoeless" Joe Jackson against the Chicago White Sox organization.

Most shocking was that the jury found in favor of Jackson, only to have the trial judge overrule their verdict. Also, included within this chapter are six internet links where the actual testimonies and legal documents from the Chicago "Black Sox" Trial of 1921, are available for viewing.

Chapter 6, *Pete Rose: An American Enigma.* It is surprising to find that so many fans get passionate about his eligibility to get into the National Baseball Hall of Fame. Many believe that both Baseball, and the NBHOF, keep manipulating and locking the admission door to keep Rose out. It is not my intention to attempt to sway readers one way or another. However, I do believe it is important that everyone be made aware of the facts. The facts, as best I could gather, along with my thoughts, are here for your reading.

Chapter 7, *Juiced: The Steroid Era,* could be a story within itself. Throughout history, baseball has had more than its fair share of scandals. But the most devastating scandal of all—doping—is rapidly dethroning the 1919 World Series as the game's worst outrage.

With the onslaught of steroids, PEDs, and other illegal stimulant drugs, a new breed of Herculean ballplayers brought forth a combination of speed and power, never before witnessed. Home runs were flying out of ballparks in record-breaking numbers, and pitchers were throwing at fireball speeds. As result, baseball's highly coveted statistical records were being left in shambles.

Doping had now moved into baseball's leadoff position. Onto the mound came the Mitchell investigation. The word was out. Jose Canseco said, "The challenge is not to find a top player who has used steroids. The challenge is to find a top player who *hasn't*." George Mitchell also named dozens of players—current and former—who had illegally used performance-enhancing drugs to different degrees. He concluded, "The illegal use of performance enhancing substances poses a serious threat to the integrity of the game."

Following closely, a multitude of baseball and other sports' star players allegedly were caught up in both the BALCO and the Biogenesis scandals. And, as for the Commissioner of MLB, and team owners, not to have noticed what was taking place? Aw... come on! They would have had to be naïve, if they thought the public didn't notice. *We* all did!

Chapter 8, *The Fork in the Road*. To a larger degree than most sports, baseball is filled with more than its fair share of cheaters, gamblers, corrupt players and top executives, illegal pill poppers, dopers, and... myths. Here, we summarize those historymaking events that embarrassed baseball, to say the least, and damaged its "clean" image among American sports. We shall also take a closer look at how the National Baseball Hall of Fame and Museum has chosen to deal with several critical issues, and see what lies ahead.

Now, the rest of the story. Enjoy!

– Jack L. Hayes

Part 1

Hijacking History

"Who controls the past controls the future. Who controls the present controls the past."

— George Orwell

Baseball's history is loaded with many heroic, heartrending, and fascinating stories. Yet, behind all the triumph and tragedy, acts of illegal gambling, game fixing, corruption, and cheating have also left their indelible marks. However, as crooked as those acts were, they failed to inflict the level of long-term damage on baseball as did those schemes contrived by three independent sources to alter the game's true history.

Chapters 1–3 address a series of conspiracies and crooked acts that altered baseball's earliest history. The National Baseball Hall of Fame and Museum also receives a black eye for their failure to right this proven wrong.[i]

Chapter 1

In Search of
Baseball's Past

"Basic honesty allows an individual to look in the mirror, and not be ashamed ever."   – Branch Rickey, Brooklyn Dodgers

In 1905 the contents of a single letter—written by a man who years later was declared a liar, alleged murderer[ii], and madman—altered the purity of America's baseball world forever.

Paternity is Everything

For over two hundred years, baseball has been called America's national pastime. Today, this game is played everywhere. I have played baseball in multimillion-dollar stadiums, schoolyards, parks and playgrounds, my grandfather's cow pasture, back alleys, and on the mall in front of the United States White House.

As a youngster, I loved baseball and gave no thought about how this game got started. Well, that was before being hired, in the early 1950s, as visiting team batboy for the Washington Senators, when

Library of Congress: 1866 Currier & Ives print of a championship game at Elysian Fields in Hoboken, N.J.

they played at home in Griffith Stadium. Then things changed.

As the batboy for each of the seven other American League teams, I got to know many of the players, and several became my heroes. Whether it was in the clubhouse, on the field or in the dugout, I became privy to a number of invaluable stories told by such old-time Hall of Famers as the great New York Yankees' catcher, Bill Dickey; baseball's premier clown, Nick Altrock; manager Casey Stengel; the legendary American and Negro League all-star pitcher, Satchel Paige; and my baseball-savvy Washington Senators' visiting team clubhouse manager, Isadore Siegel. It was through these connections I became intrigued with the game, and wanted to learn as much as possible about the history of Major League Baseball.

My clubhouse manager, "Siegel"—likely in his 80s when I knew him—was a wealth of information. He didn't just tell me credible stories of the far-distant past well before the Hall of Fame, Babe Ruth, and the dead-ball era. Siegel challenged me to learn—acting somewhat like a school teacher. I remember that during one of my first "Siegel assignments," he told me that to better understand the game's evolution I should start by learning about its beginning.

Well, with a somewhat know-it-all attitude you might expect from a teenage kid I responded, "Abner Doubleday invented baseball in Cooperstown, New York." Siegel, without saying a word, looked at me in a way I shall never forget.

Then, in the tradition of a helpful mentor, Siegel told me he wanted me to go to a library and learn how five men—Abner Doubleday, Albert Spalding, Henry Chadwick, Alexander Mills, and Abner Graves—are connected. I had my perception of the role Doubleday played; Spalding, I related to being a wealthy sporting goods manufacturer. I had never heard of Chadwick, Mills, and Graves. Siegel said it was important for me to get an overview of the role each of these men played at the start of organized baseball in America. He said the two of us would talk later, after I had completed my "homework."

Our family—after moving around Washington, D.C. three times— ended up in a small apartment above Sam's Bakery, in the 200 block of Pennsylvania Avenue, S.E. One of the best things about our apartment was its location; across the street from the United States Library of Congress. Therefore, my access to baseball history books was easy. So, across the street I went. After a couple hours of research, I understood why Siegel had given me that assignment. The game's true origin was much more complicated than I had ever imagined. *But how could this be?*

Once back in the clubhouse at Griffith Stadium, I couldn't wait to tell Siegel what I had discovered after only spending a couple hours in the Library of Congress. Siegel, the wise old man he was, listened as I excitedly described my findings. During our discussion, relating to what I had unexpectedly learned about each of the five men, I admitted that I continued to be puzzled about how—each with diverse backgrounds—they could have played such important roles, negatively impacting the true history of baseball.

Siegel's response was simple. "That's it!" His voice level reached a couple decibels higher. "That's what your quest is all about; myth versus truth." Sadly, I never got to sit down and give Siegel an update on my future discoveries. He died of a heart attack at his home in Florida, just prior to the start of the 1954 Major League Baseball season.

Myths: an American Tradition

I didn't realize it back then, but Siegel's "myth versus truth" challenge would carry me not only for days, months, one baseball season to the next, but well into my adulthood.

As I was preparing to write this chapter, I overheard a radio broadcaster talking about what he termed, as today's new phenomenon of "fake news." Well, that announcer's statement about us now living in a "post-truth" world, where the facts and experts can no longer be trusted, was also fake news. The annals of our country's history contain many incredible myths (fake news) that have wormed their way into our history books. Just think back. I bet you can quickly name a few. Three of the more famous myths that come to my mind: George Washington and his cherry tree, Paul Revere's midnight ride, and Betsy Ross and her American flag.

So why shouldn't we expect to discover a few eye-opening baseball-related myths? Well, those historians and writers charged with capturing the origin of baseball didn't let us down.

In the six-plus decades since Siegel's passing, I've discovered that if baseball advocates ever wove a mythical web, they certainly did so early in the twentieth century. Some of those stories—or should I have said "myths"—about the origin of baseball escalated my curiosity.

This inspired me to look into why and how such far-fetched tales were created. With that said, I should mention that one of my most intriguing little nugget discoveries of baseball's mythical past revolved around a well-concocted story by Abner Graves.

Shortly after the story made newspaper headlines on April 5, 1905, several qualified critics challenged what Graves had claimed pertaining to Abner Doubleday being the inventor of baseball. However, many people, particularly Americans, wanted to believe the story. If true, it would play an instrumental role in helping to validate that the game of baseball was of American origin.

Yet, with all of his bizarre baggage, Graves' shrewdly devised tale had forever altered the history of the game and its alleged birthplace, Cooperstown, New York. Even today there remains much speculation and controversy about the origin of this sport.

For example, ask any American-born individual the question, *Who invented baseball?* And even though you may hear differences of opinion as to the inventor's name, there will be little doubt the originator was an American. Now, ask that same question of a sports-minded Englishman, and don't be surprised to find a line of reasoning that baseball evolved from a game of English origin, most likely "rounders."

As for me, I had spent several years—too many, I think—being brainwashed into believing Abner Doubleday was the inventor of America's national pastime; baseball.

But, what is the real story? Unable to resist the temptation of finding out the correct answer to my self-imposed question, I returned to the libraries, bookstores, and internet. Within those resources, I found a huge selection of information; both accurate and inaccurate. Storyteller after storyteller had documented all sorts of narratives relating to baseball's beginnings. So much information about the past was so skillfully stitched together that I felt as if I could close my eyes and travel back in time—specifically to the late 1800s and into the mid 1900s.

Come, travel with me as we search for the truth.

The Journey

New York City, New York, April 6, 1889

Albert Goodwill Spalding and his two big league teams, the Chicago White Stockings and a second handpicked team of professionals—playing under the name All-America's—have just returned from their enormously successful five-month, seventeen-country, world baseball tour, promoting American goodwill and the sport of baseball.

Spalding, a former all-star baseball pitcher, team manager/owner, and wealthy co-founder of the A.G. Spalding Sporting Goods Company, was now recognized as the game's greatest visionary and supporter. He had revitalized the game of baseball in America, and his global tour had also raised the sport's reputation to higher standards worldwide.

Delmonico's Steakhouse, New York City, April 8, 1889

"A.G.," as his friends called him, was all smiles as he walked into New York City's most famous restaurant, Delmonico's Steakhouse. This visit was the first in a series of city stops to celebrate the success of his international baseball exhibitions that took place between October 1888 and April 1889.

After being greeted at the reception desk, the *maître-d'* escorted his distinguished guest to the closed entry door of the magnificently designed private dining room. With a brief hesitation—and as if on cue—the *maître-d'* took hold of the door's ornate handle and flung it wide open in a grand manner. As Spalding entered, he was met with a spectacular round of applause as all of the 300 invited guests

8

rose to greet their national hero. Making his way to the head table, A.G. paused to shake hands or say a word or two. Already seated at his table were Teddy Roosevelt, Mark Twain, and his dear friend, Abraham Mills. Those at the adjoining tables were comprised of acquaintances and admirers including baseball executives, local politicians, and prominent members of the New York Stock Exchange.

Flyer for Spaulding's Australian Base Ball Tour.

A.G., without making it obvious, was scanning the room. Missing was his English-born friend and preeminent American baseball writer and author[iii], Henry Chadwick. Henry's absence was odd since he had recently written an article for a national newspaper praising Spalding's tour as "the greatest event in the modern history of athletic sports." Chadwick was also the editor of *A.G. Spalding's Official Base Ball Guide*, and had held that position for nearly a decade. A.G. was troubled by Henry's absence.

After dinner, the master of ceremonies, Abraham Mills, called the meeting to order. Although somewhat breaking formal protocol, Mills couldn't resist commenting about the potency of his alcoholic drink before asking his dear friend to stand for a toast. With glasses raised, praise revolved around the success of the honored guest's world baseball tour. A.G. responded to the accolades in a most thoughtful and dignified manner.

As speaker after speaker took the podium, the talks focused on baseball's growth in America and how Spalding, and his tour, had not only taught this amazing sport to people in those seventeen countries visited, but had also done a great job promoting America's friendship and goodwill.

As the evening progressed, and the whiskey flowed, A.G.—a teetotaler—noticed the "tone" of several of the attendees was becoming somewhat rebellious. A series of rousing chants—"No rounders! No rounders!"—were shouted during ill-chosen times. This adage was the cry of those dead set in proving the game of baseball originated in America.

A.G. was now acutely aware of why Henry Chadwick was not present at this banquet honoring him; he was likely not invited. Henry was always going overboard in advocating that baseball evolved from the British game of rounders; not something loyal American baseball fans wanted to hear.

conflict of orgin (how the starting of American era of baseball was problematic)

"No rounders!"

This display of patriotism—although somewhat rowdy—by those attending the banquet at Delmonico's fascinated Spalding. As he and his entourage moved from city to city, A.G. noticed that during each of the pre-planned celebratory stops—as at Delmonico's— those "No rounders!" chants were growing common.

This spur-of-the-moment catchphrase pleased Spalding since he had carried on a friendly debate for over two years with Chadwick. A quick thought came to mind: *Could someone in my party be encouraging them?*

However, in 1903, the debate between the two men would turn adversarial. Chadwick published, what Spalding interpreted as unscrupulous, a nationally distributed newspaper article theorizing the British connection to baseball. Spalding vehemently disagreed. He responded harshly with a strong rebuttal; insisting that baseball was invented and first played in America.

Seeds of Truth—Layers of Deceit

At this point that once friendly debate between Spalding and Chadwick had reached the boiling point; it became a put-up or shut up challenge. In search of a way to resolve their dispute once and for all, the two men agreed to appoint a commission to investigate and learn the facts about the birth of baseball. Spalding said, "Let us appoint a commission to search everywhere possible and thus learn the truth concerning the origin and development of the game. I will abide by such a commission's findings, regardless." Chadwick also agreed.

In 1905, the Mills Commission—consisting of seven renowned sports executives—was formed. As the Commission's name implied, Abraham G. Mills was named the chairman. (Yes, the same Abraham Mills who had served as master of ceremonies at the banquet honoring Spalding at Delmonico's Steakhouse in New York City in 1889.)

One of the strategies the Commission used to trace down baseball's origin was to place a series of advertisements in nationally distributed newspapers and sports publications. The ads asked those with knowledge about the formation of the game to come forth.

Many fruitless responses were received, except for one mind-blowing letter. Its content demanded center stage attention!

"Abner Doubleday Invented Base Ball," the young newspaper vendor shouted as he waved the Tuesday, April 4, 1905, edition of the Ohio *Akron Beacon Journal* newspaper in the air. With that bold and attention-getting headline, the *Journal's* editors knew they had produced a front-page story that would likely become their month's best seller.

Amazingly, this article was based solely upon information contained in a typewritten letter to the editor, dated April 3, 1905, which had been dropped off by an unknown person at the newspaper's front desk.

The carefully worded letter noted that it was in response to an article by Albert G. Spalding seeking information as to the "origin of base ball [sic]." The letter carried the name and signature of Abner Graves, a mining engineer from Denver, Colorado.

Abner Graves

[Note: In the game's earliest years, the word "baseball" was written as two words, "base ball."]

Graves was precise when describing what he had witnessed as a five-year-old boy. He also estimated Doubleday's age, at that time, to be sixteen or seventeen. Graves closed his letter with the following paragraph: "Base ball is undoubtedly a purely American game, and its birthplace Cooperstown, New York, and Abner Doubleday is entitled to [the] first honor of its invention."

[A copy of this letter, and the November 17, 1905, letter can be found in the Author's Notes section in the back of this book.]

As you might expect, A.G. Spalding, Mills and the rest of the Commission were ecstatic when they received their copies of the *Akron Beacon Journal's* article.

The second letter from Graves, dated November 17, 1905, was sent directly to A.G. Spalding at his New York City address. This latest letter described, in even greater detail, the rules and components of Doubleday's game, including the number of players and positions, and description of the internal materials of the ball. Graves also described how Doubleday made a diagram in the dirt with a stick, and also drew on paper a layout simulating the first baseball diamond, with four bases at the corners.

The two letters were released for public viewing in July 2001 by the National Baseball Hall of Fame and Museum. This organization had obtained possession of the original letters after they were removed from scrapbooks owned by Albert G. Spalding, after his death.

The Game's Epitaph

As the Commission's research moved into its final stages, and despite all conflicting statements and unanswered questions that had surfaced over the content of the two Graves' letters, it became a foregone conclusion—strongly supported by A.G. Spalding in his July 28, 1907, letter addressed to the Special Base Ball Commission: "While it is to be regretted that the beginning of Base Ball is more or less shrouded in mystery, I believe ample evidence has been collected that will convince the most skeptical that Base Ball is entirely of American origin, and had its birth and evolution in the United States."[iv]

After three unproductive years were spent in a nationwide search, Graves had served up exactly what the Commission (and A.G. Spalding) wanted; the game was of American origin.

Various documents discovered later, would reveal that the Mills Commission had ignored making any effort to scrutinize Graves' written claim or to meet with him.

The Decision

On December 30, 1907, with his Commission's mandate set to expire, Alexander Mills wrote an eight-paragraph summation letter to Mr. James E. Sullivan, Secretary of the Special Base Ball Commission. The contents of this document would become known as the *Mills Commission Report*. Mill's closed his letter with:

"My deductions from the testimony submitted are:

First: That "Base Ball" had its origin in the United States.

Second: That the first scheme for playing it, according to the best evidence obtainable to date, was devised by Abner Doubleday at Cooperstown,

N.Y., in 1839."

Historical Facts

Below are three facts, according to my research:

1. There is no verifiable evidence that Abner Doubleday ever had any contact with, or exposure to, the game of baseball, nor did he ever mention baseball in any of his personal writings.

2. Doubleday never set foot in the village of Cooperstown during the period Graves described. He was attending West Point and later graduated in 1842. Abner Doubleday rose through the military ranks to major general during the Civil War; retiring in 1873. He died in New Jersey on January 26, 1893.

3. Some fourteen years after his death, Abner Doubleday became best known as the inventor of baseball, thanks to Abner Graves, A.G. Spalding, and the Mills Commission. The title, "Father of Modern Baseball," was bestowed on him.

As John Thorn, baseball's official historian, said, "Abner Doubleday didn't invent the game of baseball. If anything, baseball invented Abner Doubleday."

Several years later, the myth of Abner Doubleday was dethroned. *So, with Abner Doubleday stripped of his title, how did Cooperstown get selected years later to become the home of the National Baseball Hall of Fame and Museum? And, who was to become baseball's new father? It all seems very confusing. Let me explain...*

Chapter 2

Cooperstown's Field of Dreams

Today, the small village of Cooperstown, New York, is so closely linked to the birthplace of baseball that few would associate it's beginning elsewhere.

Times of Yore

The village of Cooperstown has an abundance of interesting true stories; it also is riddled with an ample amount of historymaking myths. Most of us associate this all-American town with baseball. The National Baseball Hall of Fame and Museum opened in Cooperstown in 1939, only a "stones-throw" from the very spot where a teenage boy drew, in the dirt, the layout of a new game called "baseball." Abner Doubleday's game would become known as "America's national pastime," or so the story goes.

But what makes Cooperstown, New York, worthy of such a significant place in baseball history?

In my attempt to answer this question, I researched what I considered three primary areas of influence:

Doubleday Field in 1919 (National Baseball Hall of Fame Library)

1. location of historic events

2. nationally recognized individuals who lived there along with historic homes or other places associated with that person

3. mythical tales that attract people from outside the area; for example, the movie, *Field of Dreams,* has inspired millions and attracted thousands of visitors to an isolated cornfield in Iowa.

So, let us pay a visit to the land that became famously known as the historic village of Cooperstown, New York. Initially, this land was inhabited by Iroquois Indians. Once the Revolutionary War got underway, and battles were taking place throughout New York and other northeastern states, tribes of Iroquois and other Indians joined together to fight in support of the British.

This unification became known as the Six Nations. It was their belief that the tribes stood a better chance of keeping their lands under the English. Only the Oneida and Tuscarora nations agreed to fight for the Americans. This decision often put themselves at odds with other tribes; pitting tribal brother against brother.

By mid-September 1779, the American's Continental Army had burned over forty Indian villages and numerous isolated homes, destroyed at least 160,000 bushels of corn, and an untold number of other vegetables and fruit. The American soldiers burned or cut down all that they could, leaving nothing for any Six Nation Indian who chose to return. Years later, Seneca chief, Cornplanter, remembered the campaign in a speech to President George Washington: "When your army entered the country of the Six Nations, we called you Town Destroyer, and to this day, when that name is heard our women look behind them and turn pale, and our children cling close to the necks of their mothers."[i]

The end of the Revolutionary War brought peace, but no victory. The colonial system favored land speculators at the expense of Indians. By 1790, the Six Nations had surrendered their hunting grounds in central New York to the white man, and they had either joined their brothers in the west, or agreed to resettlement on reservations within the state.[ii] Upstate New York was now the new nation's frontier. The Iroquois' domains rapidly passed to land speculators, and later to settlers.

It was during this period that William Cooper—father of James Fenimore Cooper, one of early America's most renowned authors— rose from meager means to a powerfully rich, famous, and aggressive land agent. Shortly after the end of the Revolutionary War, Cooper acquired forty to fifty thousand acres within the borders of New York State. He founded a village near Otsego Lake, later named Cooperstown, and moved his family there on November 10, 1790. In 1791, the NY governor named Cooper the presiding judge of Otsego courts—in spite of his scant education, colloquial speech, and rough manners. Three years later Cooper was elected to the U.S. Congress, winning a remarkable 84 percent of the vote in his home county. In 1799 he resigned as a judge and announced his retirement from Congress, after his Federalist party suffered catastrophic defeats brought about, in part, by his blunders. Cooper never again held a political or judicial post.

Another prominent villager was Elihu Phinney. He set up a printing press and published the village's first newspaper in 1795. Next came the *Phinney Almanac* and Bibles; found in every home. Phinney and his sons turned their business into an empire.

Next to discover and join the small enclave located alongside Otsego Lake, prior to the Civil War, was Edward C. Clark. Initially, Clark's intention was to build a summer mansion in Cooperstown. But he and his wife, Caroline, fell in love with the village, and became year-round residents, relocating from New York City.

After leaving his law practice in New York City, Clark had partnered with Isaac Singer, the inventor of the Singer Sewing Machine. In exchange for half ownership of Singer's new company, Clark helped turn the invention into the Model T of sewing machines; cheap, well built, and profitable. He also enhanced his wealth by investing heavily in Manhattan real estate; here again, his payback was substantial.

As businesses grew, more families brought their trades and wares to Cooperstown. In 1790, there were 1,702 inhabitants within Otsego County. In 1800 the population was nearly 22,000, and by 1810—one year after William Cooper's death—it was 39,000. Population increased in the county through the next two decades, but at a diminishing rate: in 1820 it stood at 45,000 and by 1830 its high point reached 51,000.

As described in his book, *A Guide in the Wilderness*, William Cooper viewed his creation of Cooperstown as the greatest justifying achievement of his life. "I began with the disadvantage of a small capital, and the encumbrance of a large family, and yet I have already settled more acres than any man in America. I am now descending into the vale of life, and I must acknowledge that I look back with self-complacency upon what I have done, and am proud of having been an instrument in reclaiming such large and fruitful tracts from the waste of the creation."[iii]

As decades passed, the publications of James Fenimore Cooper's highly popular books helped to establish Cooperstown both as a tourist center and summer resort. Leading the tourism influx were large groups of individuals looking to rediscover those places they had vicariously experienced when reading *The Pathfinder, The Pioneers, The Deerslayer,* and *The Last of the Mohicans.* Cooperstown's popularity increased in 1911when the newly founded Boy Scouts of America picked Lake Otsego as that year's campground; much of the scouts' time was devoted to readings and discussions surrounding Cooper's novels.

As the village grew, so did its need for financial help. Coming to its rescue was the Clark family. Upon Edward C. Clark's death in 1882, his four young grandsons had inherited a large share of his multimillion dollar fortune. By the 1930s, two of the grandsons— Stephen C. and Edward S.—had become exceptionally active in helping to develop Cooperstown at their own expense. The two men built a variety of first-rate buildings, including a large hotel, stone dairy complex, hospital, recreation center, and office building. Following the death of his brother Edward, in 1933, Stephen, a noted art collector and philanthropist, dedicated his life to helping with the betterment of the village he loved so dearly.

Managing the village's finances was always an area that received priority attention from Stephen Clark. Farming was now the economic mainstay and the primary income was derived from a flower known as hops—a flavoring and stability agent—primarily used in brewing beer. However, the implementation of prohibition laws, along with a plant disease identified as "blight," destroyed the economic importance of the hop fields.

With the hops market devastated, Stephen Clark believed that his only alternative was to increase the number of tourists visiting this isolated village. Unfortunately, Cooperstown was again slammed with another damaging blow when the Depression forced cancellation of the Delaware & Hudson passenger train service. Without this mode of transportation, only a dribble of wealthy visitors continued to use the village of Cooperstown as their summer getaway.

Stephen Clark—a wealthy, proven marketer, and entrepreneur—was far from throwing in the towel. Day and night, along with his trusted aide, Alexander Cleland, he pondered a variety of possibilities. Cleland, while not much of a baseball fan, became fixated on Cooperstown's best recognized claim to fame: baseball.

Igniting America's Interest

"Whoever wants to know the heart and mind of America had better learn baseball... the rules and realities of the game—and do it by watching first some high school or small-town teams."[iv]

James Fenimore Cooper's writings helped to play a pivotal role in bringing Cooperstown to the nation's forefront. But nothing did more to spark America's interest, and alter the history of that small village, than did the tale of a young man named Abner Doubleday.

As the story goes, in 1839, Doubleday was sitting in Elihu Phinney's cow pasture. A game of town ball was in progress between Otsego Academy and Green's Select School, when Doubleday described to a group of young players, the rules and layout for a new game he had invented called "base ball."

In 1935, as if by divine providence, Stephen Clark's interest in baseball was elevated when he became aware of what initially appeared to be a trivial discovery, that had taken place in the nearby hamlet of Fly Creek. An old baseball was reportedly found in the attic of the former home of Abner Graves. Stephen Clark recognized Graves' name, and knew that he was the old gentlemen who had gained national attention when the Mills Commission validated his story claiming that Abner Doubleday was the inventor of baseball in the village of Cooperstown. Clark was also well aware that Graves' Doubleday tale had been widely challenged and discredited by a number of historians and baseball experts.

Up to this point, Stephen Clark had little interest in local baseball or the Doubleday tale. But circumstances were different now; Cooperstown's economy was on the brink of failure and needed a quick infusion. *That's it! This may well be the answer to saving our village.* Stephen Clark's marketing instincts kicked in as he headed to the nearby hamlet of Fly Creek to hear firsthand what the ball's finder had to say.

Clark listened to the farmer's tale about rummaging through the attic and discovering an old trunk. Inside, the farmer said, he found some old pictures and books, and a dirty old and raggedy baseball. As Clark surmised from the appearance and amount of accumulated dust, the trunk hadn't been opened for decades. He knew almost instantly that discovery of this old, battered, and soiled baseball could be used in a campaign to add credibility to the Mills Commission's findings, and also help with the confirmation that Doubleday Field was the site of the first baseball game.

On the spot, Stephen Clark—one of America's wealthiest art collectors—understood the potential value of such a relic. He purchased the ball for five dollars, and knew exactly what he was going to do with it.

The Old "Doubleday" Baseball

The ball would be enclosed in a glass case and placed on the fireplace mantle in the Village Club's library for public viewing. While there was no proof to support the speculation, word spread that this ball was the one used by Abner Doubleday when he invented the game of baseball. As Clark expected, the locals flocked to view the Doubleday ball.

Cleland's Brainstorm, Fisk's Vision

Alexander Cleland, an advisor to the Clark family, left a routine meeting of Clark House, a family charitable foundation, on Sunday, May 6, 1934. He walked past Doubleday Field where a construction crew was filling and grading the lot. He stopped to say "Hello." During their conversation, one of the workers casually mentioned the excitement going around town about the upcoming centennial celebration of Cooperstown being the birthplace of baseball, scheduled for 1939.

After boarding the train back to his home in New York City, Cleland, always looking for business opportunities, focused on baseball: the Doubleday tale, that old ball on display in Village Club's library and the surprising number of curious visitors. Now the excitement reflected in thet workers comments about Doubleday Field were enough to get his juices flowing. Just as James Fenimore Cooper's stories had turned Cooperstown into a destination for tourists, Cleland knew that with financial help from his boss, Stephen Clark, he could do the same. Alexander Cleland became both confident and excited as he commenced to visualize his plan; the goal would be to turn Cooperstown into a baseball mecca.

Cleland wasted no time in beginning to put his plan on paper. He defined a number of critical aspects, including ways to attract a great deal of publicity, projected construction and maintenance costs for a proposed museum, and closed by citing the positive economic impact that throngs of visitors would have on the local shops, hotel, and eateries. With his plan finalized, Cleland wrote a memorandum to Stephen Clark and attached his action plan. Without hesitation, Clark approved, having long surmised that tourism was the key to

Ford C. Frick is one of the people credited with creating the Baseball Hall of Fame. Frisk held baseball-related positions as president of the National League (1934-1951) and Commissioner of Baseball (1951-1965).

enhancing the village's economic status.

Once notified of Clark's decision, Cleland, as if on a mission, would spend a large portion of his time collecting memorabilia and working with Clark to finalize plans for the much anticipated baseball museum. Naturally, that old "Doubleday" ball would become the focal point.

Cleland knew what had to take place. He had to meet with the National League President, Ford Frick, and explain the concept. In the spring of 1935, Cleland's meeting with Frick was scheduled, and Cleland presented an in-depth proposal, including Cooperstown's pledge of limited financing to host a Major League All-Star Game celebrating baseball's upcoming centennial.

Frick listened and showed casual interest in what was being said. Once the presentation ended, he enthusiastically responded, "Hell, why do that? If you're going to do that, why not start a baseball

On January 29, 1936, the U.S. Baseball Hall of Fame inducted its first members: L-R: Ty Cobb, Babe Ruth, Honus Wagner, Christy Mathewson, and Walter Johnson.

museum, a Hall of Fame, and have something that will last."[v]

With Frick's backing, a committee was formed shortly afterward to plan the celebration of baseball's centennial, culminating in the dedication of the new Hall of Fame in Cooperstown. On June 12, 1939, the National Baseball Hall of Fame held its grand opening. One of the Hall's premier artifacts was that ragged, old ball, with its cloth stuffing that resembled soiled yarn showing through the ripped cross-seam, and its cover dark enough to resemble a fossilized chaw of tobacco. Yet, that old ball was destined to become famously known as the "Doubleday" baseball.

Alexander Cleland worked the next few years pulling together the museum's collection and soliciting prominent players for memorabilia. His first response came from pitching great, Cy Young, in 1937. Young provided several keepsakes; the ball he used in 1908 to win his 500th game, various photographs, and a uniform he wore while with the Boston Braves. Other players, including Ty Cobb, followed by sending various memorabilia.

Once the backing and support of National and American League's presidents, Ford Frick and William Harridge, and the Commissioner of Baseball, Kenesaw Mountain Landis, was publicized, numerous other player and game related collectible items were received. Major League Baseball also contributed $100,000 for construction of the Hall's library wing, and for a nationwide publicity campaign.

Four of the "First Five" inductees attended the Hall of Fame's official induction ceremony on June 12, 1939, in Cooperstown. The only one missing was Christy Mathewson, who had died of tuberculosis on October 7, 1925.

The Hall's Founding Father

Just as there is no clear inventor of the game of baseball, there is no clear "founding father" of the National Baseball Hall of Fame and Museum. Yet, according to a Museum plaque, the title of *Founder of the Baseball Hall of Fame* is bestowed on Ford Christopher Frisk.

But wait, what about that virtually unknown man, Alexander Cleland? Without Cleland, it is highly probable there would not be a National Baseball Hall of Fame—at least not in Cooperstown. As noted a few pages back, Cleland knew little about baseball, but was a top-notch businessman who was struck with the brilliant idea that Cooperstown was a prime location to become the site of a baseball museum. No, not a Hall of Fame, but a museum housing all sorts of interesting baseball memorabilia, surrounding that old baseball his boss had in his possession.

Powerful Combination

Frick's vision for a Hall of Fame, combined with Cleland's dream of a baseball museum, proved to be a compelling combination.

Doubleday Field, Cooperstown, N.Y., Cavalcade of Baseball, June 12, 1939.

As a businessman, Cleland's initiative revolved around improving the economic conditions of Cooperstown. He already had three critical factors in place: claim as birthplace of baseball, that old ball, and "Doubleday" field. As for Frick, he was a true believer in the Doubleday tale. An easy solution, particularly with the financial support of the Clark family, Cooperstown was the most logical site.

Alexander Cleland became the first executive secretary for the site's operation. He worked much of the 1930s assembling his collection, overseeing construction, and managing a host of other duties ahead of Cooperstown's first induction day in 1939. He served as the first executive secretary of the National Baseball Hall of Fame and Museum from 1935 until his retirement in 1941. He died in 1954, at age 77, and has long faded from the public's memories.

Ford C. Frick served as president of the National League from 1934 to 1951. He became Commissioner of Baseball in 1951 and retired from that position in 1965. He was inducted into the National Baseball Hall of Fame and Museum in 1970. Frick, who was also a sportswriter and sportscaster, became the namesake for the Ford C. Frick Award, given to outstanding Hall of Fame broadcasters.

He died on April 8, 1978, at age 83.

The National Baseball Hall of Fame and Museum never enshrined Abner Doubleday in its hallowed quarters. His mythical tale is preserved by what a 1936 *New York Sun* editorial called an "innocuous conspiracy." Furthermore, the National Baseball Hall of Fame and Museum no longer owns the "Birthplace of Baseball" trademark, which according to the United States Patent and Trademark Office, was canceled in 2005.[vi]

The National Baseball Hall of Fame and Museum was built in Cooperstown, New York on a foundation of myth, based upon only two letters from Abner Graves,[vii] an alleged liar and madman, and an old baseball found in an attic. However, from such fake beginnings, a nearly sacred shrine in an almost perfect setting was created.

It's amazing that something so wrong would become so acceptable in the hearts and minds of Americans.

Chapter 3

Dismantling the
Cartwright Legend

"Discoveries are made by those who got there first, though they are often credited to those who got there loudest and with great support."

– Unknown

Hummm... here it is, my first trip to the National Baseball Hall of Fame and Museum in Cooperstown, New York. After taking just ten steps inside of the Plaque Gallery, I come to a sudden stop. There, mounted in front of me is a bronze plaque with the name Alexander Joy Cartwright.

It wasn't the plaque itself that startled me. It was the engraved inscription, "Father of Modern Baseball," along with three game rules crediting Cartwright as their creator: "Set bases 90 feet apart; established 9 innings as game; and 9 players as team." The plaque also honored Cartwright for introducing baseball to the Pacific Coast and Hawaii.

What the heck is going on here? Those inscription credits engraved on Cartwright's plaque are inaccurate; if not outright lies. But without them, Cartwright's plaque wouldn't be here, nor would he have a street and a park in Honolulu, Hawaii, named after him. As a historical figure, hundreds of tourists and locals pay homage at his Honolulu gravesite on an annual basis.

As I moved from one hallowed artifact to the next, I couldn't get those haunting words, "Father of Modern Baseball," out of my mind. Curiosity got the best of me. *Had I stumbled upon another misleading tale, perhaps akin to the decades' old Doubleday myth?*

With that question uppermost in mind, I was confronted with another: *Why would the National Baseball Hall of Fame and Museum's Board of Directors have allowed a plaque—containing such inaccuracies—to remain in place when every word of importance was confirmed as bogus by a variety of qualified historical experts, including John Thorn, Major League Baseball's preeminent historian?* [i]

Unbelievable! The mecca of baseball has a serious historical imperfection and, worst of all, I suspect they know this flaw exists.[ii]

Well, my next finding was almost as disappointing as the above; this time it focused on the 83rd Congress of the United States. During my research I came across several publications citing variations of the following: "On June 3, 1953, the U.S. Congress cited the research of New York City librarian Robert Henderson that clearly proved Alexander Cartwright had founded the game of baseball, and not Abner Doubleday. Henderson's book *Bat, Ball and Bishop*, which was published in 1947, documented Cartwright's contribution to the origins of the game."[iii]

Here again, another widely circulated myth. In 1953, I was associated with Major League Baseball, and my dad was an employee of the 83rd U. S. Congress; neither of us was aware of such a claim. In addition, my confirmation research found no reference in the *Congressional Record* (the official source of actions voted on by Congress) suggesting that any recognition was given to Henderson or Cartwright in 1953, or during any other Congress.

Blurred Lines

Doubleday's mythical story, the tale of an old baseball making its way into Cooperstown, the embellished creation of a larger-than-life hero, and the artful blurring of baseball and business—all of it hogwash.

Yet as fans, we love baseball and it fabrications; they are both so... American. It could be said that baseball is made up of equal portions of Abe Lincoln's honesty and P. T. Barnum's showmanship.

Decades ago, my old Washington Senators clubhouse boss convinced me to study the game's history if I wanted to learn the truth about Major League Baseball. *And, that I did.*

By the early 1900s, the tangled history of baseball was even more tangled than ever.

Gamblers had weaseled their way into various team's locker rooms and enticed a few players to "heave" a game or two. Clubhouse secrecy was in; partying, infidelity or other offensive behavior by players stayed buried in the privacy of locker rooms.

But by far, the game's biggest attention-getter was the growing controversy surrounding baseball's ancestry. Accomplishments like Cy Young (May 5, 1904) pitching the first perfect game since 1880, didn't matter; Ty Cobb's big league debut in 1905 and recognition that, by 1907, he would be the game's greatest superstar, didn't matter.

Nor did Albert G. Spalding's world exhibition tour with his two teams gaining the level of international attention they deserved. Like the others, it didn't matter. ***But, baseball's ancestry mattered.***

The Quest

The quest to find the real birthplace and inventor of baseball had taken center stage. Americans wanted to stake their claim on this game being the embodiment of our national pastime. As described in Chapter 1, what was once a little more than casual rhetoric about baseball's ancestry—be it British or American—had evolved into an all-out war of words between sportswriter Henry Chadwick and entrepreneur Albert Spalding.

On the American front, the "No rounders!" controversy was growing stronger. Chadwick held firm to his British ancestral theory. Because of the conflict between these two men and their supporters, the Mills Commission was established in 1905. Its goal was to identify once and for all, the true origin of baseball.

By the mid-1900s, with Abner Doubleday's invention of baseball in a cow pasture in upstate New York was so thoroughly debunked (by credible historians and academics), that it has taken a position in the temple of great American myths, alongside George Washington's cherry tree, Paul Revere, and Johnny Appleseed.[iv]

Replacing the Doubleday myth was the Alexander Joy Cartwright fable. He was credited with developing several rules of the modern game in New York City in the 1840s, and with helping to form the New York Knickerbockers. His staunch supporters developed a promotional plan of attack that would make any politician running for office envious. The "Vote Cartwright into the Hall of Fame" faction were hell-bent on accomplishing their goal. For example, Bruce Cartwright Jr. vowed he would do whatever necessary to get his grandfather inducted into this national memorial; *from what I found, he did a splendid job.*

During my research, it was interesting to note that, while several historians had gone to extremes in pointing out questionable issues found within the Doubleday assertion, those same "experts" moved to proclaim Alexander J. Cartwright, the first bona fide architect of American baseball. To them, it didn't matter that those four contributions engraved on Cartwright's plaque brought forth their very own suspicious luggage; worthy of a challenge.

Cartwright, unlike Doubleday, had the credentials to prove he played baseball, and was a member of a credible baseball team; the New York Knickerbocker Club. As Cartwright's Hall of Fame plaque signifies, he received the ultimate recognition for his contributions to baseball when inducted into the National Baseball's Hall of Fame and Museum in 1938.

Fading Glory

In my quest to learn as much as possible about Alexander J. Cartwright, the deeper I dug into baseball's past, the more I began to suspect that his story could also be a mythical tale, similar to the Doubleday falsehood; just the names changed.

As for the two men, we know Abner Doubleday and Alexander Cartwright had at least four things in common:

- They had never met

- Both were declared America's inventor of baseball

- After death, both had their identities hijacked by unscrupulous advocates filled with deceitful motives

- Each went to their grave never knowing about being named the "Father of Baseball"

Other than the above, contrasts between the two men were astounding. For example, Abner Doubleday was a Major General in the U.S. Army, and his only documented connection to baseball took place in 1871: As commanding officer of the 24th Infantry Regiment at Fort McKavett, Texas, Doubleday made a formal request to his superior officer for the purchase of various items, including baseball implements for the amusement of his men.

Alexander Cartwright was just the opposite. He was a member of the New York Knickerbocker Baseball Club during the mid-nineteenth century.

In 1866, Charles A. Peverelly, author of *Book of American Pastimes,* credited "Cartwright in the spring of 1845, as proposing a regular baseball organization, and promising to obtain several recruits." Miscellaneous findings and a scorecard notation indicated that on June 19, 1846, Cartwright may have umpired the first match game using the new Knickerbocker rules. The Knicks lost that game to the New York Ball Club by a score of 23–1 in four innings.

There is no documentation indicating that Cartwright was a principal influence with the New York Knickerbockers, let alone as the game's sole inventor. "Cartwright won his plaque in the Baseball Hall of Fame primarily through the efforts of his son Bruce, and more importantly, those of grandson Bruce Jr."[v]

As noted in Chapter 1, we now have a good handle on the Abner Doubleday myth, and those who contrived it. *But, what do we REALLY know about Alexander Joy Cartwright and those who manufactured his claim to fame?*

This question would become the driving force behind this chapter.

Creating a Legend

To understand the rise of Alexander Joy Cartwright, becoming a baseball legend worthy of earning a place in the National Baseball Hall of Fame and Museum, we must travel back to the nineteenth century. Just as Abner Graves was instrumental in catapulting Abner Doubleday into baseball's history books, three men played prominent roles in helping Cartwright:

- William Rankin
- Bruce Cartwright Sr.
- Bruce Cartwright Jr.

William Rankin

William Rankin was an up-and-coming sportswriter. By the 1870s, he was in New York, freelancing as a junior sports reporter; often writing baseball columns for a variety of newspapers. By the early 1900s, as the senior New York correspondent for the *Sporting News*, he was writing weekly baseball columns. On January 15, 1905, while preparing an article on the Mills Commission asking for help from the public regarding the origin of baseball, Rankin was reminded of his 1877 interview with the former Knickerbocker player and first Knickerbocker Club president, Duncan Curry.

That interview was filled with possibilities capable of resolving this investigation, Rankin thought. Known for his meticulously kept scrapbook on baseball, it was an easy matter for Rankin to locate his file: Duncan Curry Interview.

Once his memory of the Curry interview was refreshed, on January 15, 1905, Rankin fired off what would become his first of three letters to the Mills Commission. (Unknown to Rankin at that time, the contents of those letters, along with his related articles, would play an instrumental role in helping to alter the history of baseball, at least for decades to come.)

Mills Commission Letters

William Rankin's initial letter to Alexander Mills contained verbatim details of his 1877 interview with Duncan Curry. He wrote:

> *"While standing near Brooklyn City Hall conversing with Robert Ferguson—a star player and manager of the day—when Ferguson pointed out a nearby gentleman, declared 'here comes one of the real fathers of Base Ball,' and introduced him to Duncan Curry. After conversing a bit, Curry asked why none of the reporters would correct the errors put forward by Henry Chadwick. Curry continued with his*

story: 'One afternoon when we had gathered on the lot for a game, someone, but I do not remember now who it was, had presented a plan, drawn up on paper, showing a ball field, with a diamond to play on— eighteen men could play at one time.

There was the catcher, the pitcher, three basemen, a short field and three outfielders. The plan caused a great deal of talk, but finally, we agreed to try it. Right here let me say the man placed at short field was then considered the least important one of the nine men. His duty was as an assistant to the pitcher. To run and get the ball thrown in from the field, or when thrown wildly by the catcher when returning it to the pitcher. It was Dick Pearce who first made the short field one of the most important on the ball field. There was one of the greatest little players that ever played ball."

(Rankin indicated this dialogue was taken from his notes written in 1877.)

Will Rankin followed his first letter with a second, dated February 15th; a follow-up to his Curry interview. Although this time it focused on his conversation with Thomas Tassie, the former president of the prominent Atlantic Club of Brooklyn, and a member of the 1857 rules committee. Rankin wrote:

"As I [Rankin] related Curry's story to Tassie about a man with a paper, Tassie broke in excitedly and confirmed the story. He also identified the man: 'I think it was a Mr. Wadsworth. Not the one who played ball, but a gentleman and a scholar who held an important position in the Customs House. He was one of the best after-dinner speakers of the day. Now, I may be wrong about that, but it is the impression I have had for many years, as I have heard that part of Base Ball's origin talked of many times."

Rankin had now identified the unknown man as a Mr. Wadsworth. (It is important to note that this Mr. Wadsworth was described by Tassie as being a gentleman and scholar; **not** the Wadsworth who played baseball.)

Rankin is clear in his second letter that his main point was to help prove that baseball did not derive from either rounders or town ball. He emphasized that the identification of baseball's inventor and dates are secondary. *"Every veteran I [Rankin] have seen since 1877 has said the same thing: 'I have never seen Rounders or Town Ball and do not know how it is played.'"*

Rankin also publicized much of the information, contained in his second letter to Mills, in a column in *The National Pastime* dated April 8, 1905. His story was a retelling of the two letters, but with expanded detail. This latest column included the following never before seen important statement by Duncan Curry: *"That was the origin of base ball and it proved a success from the start."*

After reading Rankin's February 15th letter, Commissioner Abraham Mills, still focusing on his task of investigating the origin of baseball, saw a connection with the information Rankin had provided. Mills became interested in interviewing "Mr. Wadsworth"; but failed to make any contact or turn up anything that would lead him to this person of interest. Mills wrote back to Rankin requesting more information. Uncertain about Mr. Wadsworth's identity, Rankin set out to investigate. After speaking with Tassie again, Rankin admitted an error must have been made. "William [Rankin] recounted the matter to Abraham Mills, perhaps on January 16, 1908."[vi]

Three years later, on April 2, 1908, Rankin would make public in *Sporting News* the identical column as previously published on April 8, 1905, but with a new spin. This time Rankin combined his conversations with Duncan Curry in 1877 and Thomas Tassie in early 1905, into a single story. Another new detail was added: Tassie had called Wadsworth "the Chauncey M. Depew (a U.S. Senator from New York noted for his oratory and after-dinner speaking) of that day."

Rankin would again write to Commissioner Mills stating that after his interview with Tassie, and while looking up records for an unrelated story, he found a letter given to him by H.G. Crickmore, a former sportswriter on the *New York World*, during the summer of 1876. On the back of the envelope, Rankin said he had written "Mr. Alex J. Cartwright, father of baseball."[viii]

Rankin said this discovery resulted in him remembering that Duncan Curry had told him it was Cartwright who had brought the plan for baseball. He said it was not Curry who had forgotten this man's identity, but it was he [Rankin]who had forgotten the name Curry had given.

Rankin said that finding that notation on the back of Crickmore's letter sparked his memory, and he "called on the editor of the *Sunday Mercury*, Mr. Cauldwell, and Cauldwell said, 'It was Cartwright who organized the old Knickerbocker Club, and it would be only natural that he had a game to play or he would not have suggested organizing a club.'"

Rankin said he continued to contact a few older players, who jointly agreed that the only Wadsworth they knew who was involved in baseball, hadn't started playing until the 1850s. (As previously documented by Rankin, Tassie had made it clear during his interview that the individual he described was *not* Wadsworth the ballplayer.)

Another of the older players, William Van Cott, confirmed, "It was Alex Cartwright who took the plans of base ball, the present game, up to the ball field and was laughed at, but he was so persistent about having his scheme tried that it was finally agreed to do so, and it proved a success from the start."

Also, according to Van Cott, it was Cartwright who suggested organizing a club to play his game. (Van Cott played baseball between the 1850s and 1860s. No record was found showing he played anytime during the 1840s when Cartwright was present.) At the time of Rankin's 1908 interview, it was established that Van Cott was old, ill and likely near death. *Is it possible Van Cott was just confirming whatever Will Rankin wanted?*

Another controversial point was when Will Rankin's obituary appeared in *Sporting Life* on April 5, 1913. The death announcement stated that Will (Rankin) "felt" that he should have had the title of "Father of Base Ball" instead of Henry Chadwick. Teddy Roosevelt was actually the one who named Chadwick the "Father of Base Ball" in his birthday wishes to the Exeter, England, native in 1904.[ix] (Historian for Major League Baseball, John Thorn, explained: "No man was more important to the rise of baseball from boys' game to national pastime than Henry Chadwick, the game's great promoter.")

The Saga Continues

Now, let us continue to examine the so-called "evidence" that led to Alexander Joy Cartwright being anointed with the National Baseball Hall of Fame and Museum's prestigious title of "Father of Modern Baseball."

Throughout history, numerous articles and books have been written about the life and legend of Alexander Joy Cartwright. It is also important to note that, prior to 1909, except for Rankin's 1877 interview with Duncan Curry, I was unable to identify any nineteenth-century writer crediting Cartwright with any of those accomplishments listed on his plaque.

As previously mentioned, there are stacks upon stacks of written materials relating to Cartwright. So much that I would have to extend this chapter by hundreds of pages, just to provide a comprehensive account of this man.

Many of the "facts" relating to Cartwright's baseball triumphs, and his trek from New York to the goldfields of California, were allegedly documented in his "Gold Rush Journal." Next, I would discover that this valuable document was intentionally burned. This important tidbit came from a reference made in Harold Peterson's 1973 book, *The Man Who Invented Baseball*. Peterson tells that, during his research phase, "one of Cartwright's sons, Bruce Cartwright Sr., had burned his father's original "Gold Rush Diary" because it contained information potentially damaging to prominent people in California and Hawaii."

During my research, I came upon another interesting and confusing thing about the original "Gold Rush Journal." Several typed transcriptions of that diary existed; each containing important, yet conflicting and unverifiable, discrepancies. As you might have already surmised, with the original journal destroyed, there is no way to confirm what Alexander Cartwright had actually recorded. In other words, I was unable to separate fact from fiction.

Therefore, after spending days on end researching and trying to confirm the accuracy of a variety of Cartwright stories, I have omitted from this chapter any narrative that does not address the reasons Cartwright was honored with the title, "Father of Modern Baseball."

Bruce Cartwright, Sr.

In 1909, Bruce Cartwright Sr., under the belief that all of the original Knickerbocker Base Ball Club players were deceased, declared that his father had been the one to invent baseball. "I remember as a child, he had among his personal belongings a baseball that he treasured very highly, stating that it was used by the Knickerbocker Club in their early games. This ball was used by myself and others in the first baseball club organized in Honolulu and was finally lost or destroyed (although it miraculously turned up at auction in 1999). My father also had at that time valuable data pertaining to the early history of the Knickerbocker Club. None of this is available today. Far out in the mid-Pacific, in this little island world of ours, it is quite natural that we should lose touch with the later progress of this noble pastime, and I can easily conceive how my father could be almost forgotten by his old-time friends in the United States."[x]

Bruce Cartwright, Jr.

Alexander J. Cartwright's story involved many individuals, some novices, and others possessing a bias. But none had the level of determination, initiative, and audacity of his grandson, Bruce Cartwright Jr.

As a youngster, Bruce Jr. was proud of his grandpa. During an interview for an article in *Paradise of the Pacific,* he told a journalist, "When I was a small boy, it was my great joy to hear grandpa tell about the early days of baseball in New York, and of his adventures while crossing the continent."

Bruce Jr. knew his grandfather had played on a baseball team stateside; the New York Knickerbocker Base Ball Club. He was only ten years old when his grandfather died on July 12, 1892. Therefore, he had no firsthand knowledge of his grandfather's baseball accomplishments.

At age fifty-four, Bruce Jr. became determined for the public to get to know his grandfather. After all, based on the stories to which he had been privy, his grandpa belonged in Baseball's Hall of Fame.

Rewriting History

Bruce Jr. had big plans for his grandfather's legend. It was important that he stay current on what was happening in the baseball circles in the States, especially if there was any information coming over the radio that would help him in his quest. There was no room for mistakes.

There had been growing controversy over Abner Doubleday being named the "Father of Baseball." A few baseball historians and sportswriters were speaking out about their concerns that the Doubleday tale was a fraud. Bruce Jr. had been keeping up on the scuttlebutt as best he could—considering he was living far away in Hawaii. Almost daily, his radio updates included a few bits and pieces about the status of the future Baseball Hall of Fame, scheduled to open in the summer of 1939.

It was no secret that both Bruce Jr., and his dad, had declared Alexander Joy Cartwright belonged in the upcoming National Baseball Hall of Fame. As stated previously, Bruce Jr. had vowed he would do whatever was necessary to get his grandfather inducted into this national memorial.

With Doubleday losing creditability almost daily, the Cartwright movement was picking up unplanned support from across the baseball world. It was a real plus when William Rankin, the popular sportswriter mentioned earlier, named Alexander J. Cartwright as "Father of Base Ball." Shortly thereafter, another well-known sports journalist, Frank G. Menke, rejected the Doubleday myth and came out in support of Cartwright.

The conditions couldn't be better; it was time for Bruce Jr. to execute the plan of action he had imagined and mentally rehearsed for years. His first step was to implement a two prong letter writing campaign. He recognized that his campaign needed credibility. So he convinced the Honolulu city manager to use official letterhead and write a letter of praise and endorsement for Alexander Cartwright. Next, Bruce Jr. wrote a series of letters promoting his grandfather's case to the Centennial Commission; these "targeted" commission members were responsible for the Hall of Fame's grand opening and inductee selection process. His correspondence included stories about his grandfather telling "many local people that he organized (the Knickerbocker team), drew up the rules they played under and also laid out the first 'baseball diamond.'" He offered A. J. Cartwright's "Gold Rush Diary" as further evidence."[xi]

Bruce Jr. was pleased with his progress. He had accomplished an important part of his goal when the Centennial Commission responded and indicated they would give preferential consideration to the induction of his grandfather, into the National Baseball Hall of Fame.

It further elated Bruce Jr., when he was notified that the 1938 Hall of Fame inductee plaque recipients would be comprised of the great Phillies pitcher, Grover Cleveland Alexander, Henry Chadwick, *AND* Alexander Joy Cartwright. Abner Doubleday's name was obviously missing from this distinguished list.

Shocking Discovery

As noted previously, Bruce Cartwright Jr. had agreed to provide the Hall of Fame's centennial commissioners with a copy of Alexander Cartwright's "Gold Rush Diary." Well, the more I researched, the greater I became confused and concerned. I was discovering what several others apparently had known for decades. There were multiple handwritten and typed transcriptions of Alexander Cartwright's original journal.

To further complicate this matter, when comparing each individual transcript to others, serious discrepancies were identified. For example, the alleged handwritten *original* journal residing in the Bishop Museum contains an undated passage, "Left Independence and traveled to the Boundary line, where we camped with Colonel Russell's Co. for over a week nothing of note occurring, time passed in "fixing" waggon [sic]covers, stowing away property & c [sic] varied by hunting, fishing, and swimming."[xii] Baseball was not mentioned in this handwritten version.

However, in the 1930s' transcription, represented to be the exact copy of Cartwright's original journal that was typed by Bruce Jr., an entry reads, "leaving New York on March 1, 1849, to travel by train to St. Louis. From St. Louis we traveled by a steamboat to

Independence, Missouri." According to another entry dated April 23, 1849, Alexander J. Cartwright wrote, "During the past week we have passed the time in fixing the wagon-covers, stowing away property etc. varied by hunting and fishing, swimming and playing Base-ball. I have the ball and book of rules with me that we used back home." Bruce Jr. also added that he completed the narrative drawn from all, available sources.[xiii]

What did others traveling on that same wagon train have to say about playing baseball?

According to author Monica Nucciarone in her 2009 book, *Alexander Cartwright, The Life Behind the Baseball Legend* (page 190), "I have attempted to find baseball references in other gold rush journals: I have not located any." Nucciarone explained that various trail associations with databases consisting of thousands of diaries and their locations, with whom she had contact, "declared that they know of no diaries mentioning baseball, including the four diaries that remain from the Newark Overland Company: those of Charles Glass Gray, Cyrus Currier, Robert Bond, and Alexander Cartwright."

Furthermore, Louis J. Rasmussen's research of diary records pertaining to the Newark Overland Company's wagon train—on which Cartwright was a passenger—concluded basically the same thing as Nucciarone; no baseball is mentioned.

Spin Zone

The more in-depth my research, the more issues of concern arose. For example, Mary Check, the granddaughter of Alexander Cartwright, went to her grave believing the handwritten journal she had bequeathed to the Bishop Museum was the original document. Ms. Check's will reads:

"I give to the Bishop Museum at Honolulu, Hawaii, the original of the diary of Alexander Joy Cartwright, Jr. as an addition to the Cartwright

Family Collection of said museum, to be designated and identified as a gift to said collection by me."[xiv]

Keep in mind that early in this chapter I noted that Harold Peterson had written in his book, *The Man Who Invented Baseball,* that Bruce Cartwright Sr., had burned his dad's original "Gold Rush Journal." Therefore, I was not surprised to learn the Bishop Museum's handwritten journal's authenticity came into question.

With the journal's originality under scrutiny, Reed Hayes, a certified document examiner from Honolulu, was retained to confirm its authenticity. After comparing several known handwriting samples of Alexander Joy Cartwright Jr. to the handwriting in the Bishop Museum's journal, Hayes determined that Cartwright was not the author of that journal. In defense, the Museum's archivist, DeSoro Brown, said that occasionally handwritten items of great importance to families were transcribed by someone else with excellent handwriting. Following the possibility provided by the archivist, that another person may have transcribed the document in question, I must ask, *why would any narrative pertaining to baseball be omitted if it appeared in the original diary?*

Alexander Joy Cartwright Jr.

Here's another peculiarity: In preparation for an article about Alexander Cartwright and the Knickerbockers in the 1947 *San Francisco News-Call Bulletin,* writer Jack McDonald spoke with a fellow reporter, Mike Jay. Jay had written a 1920s article about Bruce Cartwright Jr. donating his grandfather's 1865 letter to former Knickerbocker teammate, Charles DeBost, to the California Archives. The two reporters met in Mike Jay's office in San Francisco.

Jay reached into a desk drawer and retrieved his copy of Alexander Cartwright's journal. A quick thumb through of the pages revealed several entries mentioning baseball. McDonald was surprised. He was familiar with the contents of the Bishop Museum's journal, and those in possession of the Cartwright family, and he knew that baseball was not mentioned. At once he knew something was amiss; the differences were glaring.[xvi]

Is it possible that Bruce Cartwright Jr. manufactured a tale similar to the one that Abner Graves used to connect baseball with a person of American heritage? Yes, possibly so. I am concerned that those baseball related stories during Cartwright's trip out west were also likely conceived and inserted into the "Gold Rush Journal" by Bruce Jr.

At the onset of this chapter, I talked about my visit to the National Baseball Hall of Fame and Museum and discovering that the Alexander Joy Cartwright plaque *wrongfully* credited Cartwright with being the "Father of Modern Base Ball."

While there is confirmation that links Cartwright to baseball and the Knickerbocker Base Ball Club of New York, there is more than enough evidence to indicate that Bruce Cartwright Sr., and his son, Bruce Jr., manipulated historical records and embellished stories in their pursuit to have Alexander Joy Cartwright be honored in the National Baseball Hall of Fame and Museum.

In addition to the questionable discrepancies noted throughout this chapter, we cannot ignore the following: "In 2016, experts including John Thorn, Major League Baseball's official historian, authenticated a set of documents titled "Laws of Base Ball" written in 1857 by New York Knickerbockers president, Daniel 'Doc' Adams, after his discussion with executives of fourteen other New York clubs.

These documents established the rules of the game, including nine innings, nine players on the field, and 90-foot base paths. Cartwright was not a participant at that 1857 meeting; he was living in Hawaii."[xvii]

These documents clearly show that Doc Adams should have been credited with those rules erroneously attributed to Alexander J. Cartwright.

No evidence, other than that submitted by Bruce Jr., was found to support the plaque's declaration that Cartwright was the person who "carried baseball to the Pacific Coast and Hawaii in the pioneer days." My findings call into question the validity of those *alleged* "Gold Rush Journal" copies submitted by Bruce Cartwright Jr. and/or others.

Conclusion: Part One

The history of baseball is like looking at a family album. It's always interesting to study a batch of old photos and wonder how well we really know the ancestral history of those we believe we knew so much about. Baseball is no different.

In *Chapter 1*, we learned the Abner Doubleday tale was an easily identifiable myth.

Below are three facts according to my research...

1. There is no verifiable evidence that Abner Doubleday ever had any contact with, or exposure to, the game of baseball; nor did he ever mention baseball in any of his personal writings.

2. Doubleday never set foot in the village of Cooperstown during the period Abner Graves, a Colorado mining engineer, described in his two 1905 letters. Doubleday was then attending West

Point and graduated in 1842. Abner Doubleday rose through the military ranks to major general during the Civil War; retiring in 1873. He died in New Jersey on January 26, 1893.

3. Some fourteen years after his death, Abner Doubleday became best known as the inventor of baseball, thanks to Abner Graves, A.G. Spalding, and the Mills Commission. The title, "Father of Modern Baseball," was bestowed on him. And then, several years later, the myth of Abner Doubleday was dethroned.

Ironically, Doubleday never knew anything about any of this.

Chapter 2: The National Baseball Hall of Fame and Museum was built in Cooperstown, New York, on a foundation of myth, based upon only a highly questionable tale by Abner Graves, and an old baseball found in an attic.

Turning that old "Doubleday" baseball, along with Phinney's cow pasture, into national relics that perfectly intertwined with Abner Graves' tale were strokes of genius. It was undertaken as a commercial venture that proved very successful.

Chapter 3 takes on the question, *is Alexander Cartwright's induction into the National Baseball Hall of Fame and Museum valid or was it another well-executed scam?*

There is sufficient evidence to show that those accomplishments— set bases 90 feet apart, established 9 innings as game and 9 players as team—listed on Cartwright's plaque are obviously false. According to verifiable documentation, the above rules were not implemented until 1857.

Cartwright left New York in 1849, never to return.

Note: As for any discrepancies found in the Hall of Fame: A placard in the Hall of Fame states that although later studies have called into question the accuracy of information on the plaques, the facts as engraved, were believed to be accurate at the time. (Therefore, I interpret this to mean that no changes will be made to correct Cartwright's plaque. Hopefully someday, Doc Adams will be recognized for his contributions.)

Another case of irony: Alexander Cartwright did not live to know that he, too, was recognized as the "Father of Baseball."

Mystery Man

Next, we should not ignore that mysterious *"someone"* who first came to light during Will Rankin's 1877 interviews with Duncan Curry and Thomas Tassie. Earlier in this Chapter 3, I cited the detailed account of Rankin's 1877 interview with Duncan Curry. Curry's remarks were: "One afternoon when we had gathered on the lot for a game, someone, but I do not remember now who it was, had presented a plan, drawn up on paper, showing a ball field, with a diamond to play on—eighteen men could play at one time." Thomas Tassie later confirmed Curry's story. He also identified the mystery man as a "Mr. Wadsworth" who held an important position in the Customs House.

Some thirty years later Rankin would go public and say he made a mistake in naming "Mr. Wadsworth" as the individual whom both Duncan Curry and Thomas Tassie were speaking of during their interviews. Rankin said that, after he found Cartwright's name scribbled on the back of an old envelope, he remembered the person both Curry and Tassie were referring to was not Mr. Wadsworth, but actually Alexander Cartwright.

Thanks to the research of John Thorn, Major League Baseball's official historian and author of *Baseball in the Garden of Eden*, the saga of the mystery man was solved. He was identified as Louis Fenn Wadsworth. As Tassie had said, Wadsworth was connected to the Customs House. However, he was the attorney, and therefore not listed as an employee.

Thorn said, "While Abraham G. Mills was searching for the baffling 'Mr. Wadsworth,' his possible trump card to Doubleday, no one connected Louis F. Wadsworth, a long-term inmate of the Plainfield Industrial Home, as being the same individual named by Thomas Tassie in connection with the Duncan Curry interview. With the death of all the Knickerbocker Base Ball Club members from their first decade of play—unbeknownst to the baseball world, Wadsworth was the last to go—no one was left to gainsay the declaration by Bruce Cartwright Sr., in 1909, that his father had been the one to invent baseball. Journalists who should have known better rallied around (Cartwright's) alternative theory in reaction to what they saw as the absurdity of the claim on behalf of Doubleday."

Rankin, by simply substituting one name with another some thirty years after his initial interviews in 1877, likely played an instrumental role in altering the history of baseball.

So many unresolved questions! It remains puzzling as to why the Centennial Commission inducted Alexander Joy Cartwright into the National Baseball Hall of Fame and Museum in 1938 without confirmation of those *"facts"* presented by Bruce Cartwright Jr.

According to one credible report, "Bruce Cartwright Jr. lobbied so hard, implying that his Honolulu allies would somehow spoil Cooperstown's Centennial of Baseball in 1939, that the Knickerbocker pioneer of indeterminate accomplishments won a place in the hallowed hall."[xviii]

Bruce Cartwright Jr. did not attend the official opening of the National Baseball Hall of Fame and Museum on June 12, 1939, or take part in the celebration of National Cartwright Day at Brooklyn's Ebbets Field on August 26, 1939. He died (age 56) on January 11, 1939.

As for the inventor of baseball, I believe sportswriter Henry Chadwick said it best back in 1898: *"Baseball never had no 'fadder'; it jest growed."*

Part Two

The Clouds of Corruption

Baseball gambling and game fixing scandals—games in which the final results have been altered due to the efforts of dishonest players, managers, or umpires—is baseball's dark side.

Gambling, game fixing, and bribery are forms of baseball's greatest nemeses. Chapters 4–6 begin the process of exploring the impact of these crimes.

Since not all scandals relate solely to game fixing and gamblers, I have included in Chapter 7, information about the facts and myths revolving around the crazy world of performance enhancing drugs and steroids, and their negative impact on Major League Baseball.

Chapter 8 is the final chapter. While it gives us a brief synopsis of what was covered in each of the prior chapters, I thought it would be interesting to also attempt to look at what lies ahead within this darker side. My projections may be a little like gazing into a crystal ball and hoping that only positive images appear—which is highly unlikely. At least, as long as money and glory are primary motivational factors.

Chapter 4

Gambling &
Game Fixing Schemes

"Any professional base ball club will 'throw' a game if there is money in it. A horse race is a pretty safe thing to speculate on in comparison with the average ball match." – Beadle's Dime Base Ball Player, 1875

Decisions, Decisions...

Today, organized baseball, along with other sports, is on the verge of entering a lucrative, chaotic and threatening new era. On Monday, May 14, 2018, in a 6–3 ruling by its justices, the United States Supreme Court demolished a 1992 federal ruling that barred betting on baseball, football, basketball, and other sports in most states. Why now? It's all about money!

In his *New York Times* column, Adam Silver put the value of illegal sports bets at $400 billion a year. With big money involved—legal or not—sports leagues and local governments want a piece of the action. Betting on baseball by professional baseball players, team and league officials, umpires, and associated employees will remain prohibited—legal or otherwise—or wagering on any sport through an illegal bookmaker.

"Before and between the innings, gamblers circulated throughout the crowd, announcing betting odds changes as the game progressed. Once the fifth inning ended, the odds shifted sharply."

Yet, sports leagues have complained about expanding any form of sports gambling. They say that such action could severely damage their huge businesses and its integrity, if fans thought someone who had wagered money on a specific result could alter the outcome of a game.

Safety and acts of retribution are also concerns. Some fans are unpredictable. I wrote in one of my earlier books, *Baseball's Finest Moments,* that as a young batboy for the Washington Senators' visiting teams, the job I hated most was troting alongside the left field stands at Griffith Stadium to retrieve the jacket of visiting team's relief pitcher when he was coming into the game. Fans would throw all types of things at me, because I was wearing the uniform of the visiting team. So, if that behavior can take place during such trivial circumstances, imagine what could happen to a player if a drunken or irate fan had put money on that player's at-bats. What if the player makes a game-turning error that causes the bettor's team to lose, or even if a home plate umpire makes a questionable call that affects a game's outcome?

The Decision

The Supreme Court's decision is monumental. Legalized sports gambling has the potential for increasing business, fueling interest in sports, creating new jobs, and generating significant tax revenue.

Promises, Promises.

Politicians are promising that all sports betting revenue destined for state coffers be earmarked for education. Unfortunately, this is not always true; sometimes that money is used for unrelated expenditures.

A CBS report "found that education spending dropped or flattened in twenty-one of the twenty-four states that earmarked lottery funds for education. Lotteries help, but not as much as you may think. Even when proceeds are earmarked for education, lotteries cover only a fraction of state education spending."

The quest for added income will be the driving force that will gain the support of local government agencies, and sports leagues (team owners and players), wanting a piece of the action. It would not surprise me to see betting windows installed in some ballparks soon, to help bring in more revenue and keep action loving fans in their seats until the game ends.

Winning or Losing

Back a couple decades, I appeared on a national TV show alongside a habitual gambler. Our topic was sports betting. Whatever your thoughts on gambling—you can take this to the bank—a lot of Americans are ruining their lives betting on, or against, their favorite team.

Nothing hits home more than the sad story of Pete Rose, but more about Pete "Charlie Hustle" Rose later. As for the integrity associated with gambling, here are two of my personal experiences: The first had to do with me stopping to say hello to a casual friend while at a local harness racing track.

As we chatted, my acquaintance quickly interrupted and said, "See that woman headed for the (betting) window. Bet on the same horse she does; she's a jockey's wife." Guess what? I did and, thanks to that unknown jockey's wife, that was my only winner that night.

Next story: One man, with whom I worked, told me his wife owned a racehorse, and they had been "holding the horse back to increase its betting odds." The horse was now ready to run, so I should bet on it. Along with three or four others in our office, I placed bets. Well, the horse got bumped when it left the gate and finished near last.

Once again, after being told that the "horse was ready to win," we made our bets. My payoff was just another excuse. The third time, well, guess what? I didn't bet. The others did; the horse won.

Those two experiences taught me a valuable lesson about gambling: I learned how to avoid letting that giant "sure thing" vacuum suck up my hard-earned cash.

The Dark Side

My two experiences have nothing to do with betting on baseball. But, they do send a clear message: Gamblers want to win—and some people will do whatever it takes to help them win. Gambling, and game fixing scandals, first wormed their way into baseball when the game was in its infancy.

At its onset, baseball was an amateur sport, played by "gentlemen" of the upper class for their enjoyment. To make their games more fun and interesting, it became common for a small wager—dinner or a tidy sum of money—to be bet on favorites.

As the popularity of baseball was spreading from community to community, it didn't take long for other classes of people to start playing, and watching, this exciting sport. For many, a small wager increased the excitement. This increasing popularity also brought with it a need to expand the number of baseball clubs.

Along with the expansions, came increases in operating costs associated with team travel and play. Club owners could no longer depend on the financial support they received from donations or sponsors. Charging admission to games became an alternative. One investor, Harry Wright, wrote, "We must make the game worth witnessing and there will be no fault found with the price. A good game is worth 50 cents, a poor one is dear at 25 (cents)."

Roll of the Dice

Those clubs determined to establish winning records, commenced making illegal *under-the-table* payments to their team's best performing players. Ignoring the rules of amateur play—by paying players—sent the message that if club owners were willing to secretly pay players to assure victory, it was also logical for gamblers to assume they could bribe players to assure defeat.

Unquestionably, baseball had become a moneymaking machine. No matter which side—clubs or gamblers—opportunities were abundant for raking in profits. On the illegal side, the games also became ripe for picking. Suspicions of illegal player bribes and game "heaves," or fixes, became public knowledge in the early 1860s.

I am a believer in that old saying, "The past is the best predictor of the future." During my research for this chapter, I found that my best resources were old newspaper articles, internet pieces, Library of Congress and public libraries, and books on a variety of scandals, most notably the notorious Chicago "Black Sox" and the 1919 World Series.

Cynicism Follows Corruption

"Baseball had, for some time, been living uneasily in the knowledge that bribes were being offered by gamblers, and that some players were accepting them. The players knew it was going on, and the owners knew it was going on. But more importantly, the players knew that the owners knew—and they knew that the owners were doing nothing about it for fear of a scandal that might damage organized baseball. Under such conditions, it quite obviously did not pay to be honest."[i]

It's no secret that some of the most talented managers, ballplayers, officials, and umpires have been involved with gamblers in one way or another, whether by throwing games or betting on a game in which they took part or controlled. Once discovered, such unscrupulous actions undermine the public's confidence in the game itself. One of the first corruption problems that came to the public's attention occurred in 1865, when a betting scandal destroyed a baseball team known as the New York Mutuals.

Game Fixing Schemes

Baseball's First Scandal

On September 28, 1865, an estimated crowd of three to four thousand filled the grounds at Elysian Fields in Hoboken, New Jersey. The game between the Eckfords of Brooklyn, and Mutuals of New York, was scheduled to get underway at 3:20 p.m.

MUTUAL NINE, 1864.

At game time, the Mutuals were the odds-on favorite to win. Therefore, it came as no surprise when the Mutuals quickly moved ahead, taking a 3–0 lead. By the end of the fourth inning, the score had narrowed to a 5–4 Mutuals' lead. In the bottom of the fifth, the Mutuals' caliber of play changed radically: "over-pitched balls, wild throws, passed balls, and failures to make easy catches in the field marked the play of the Mutuals to an unusual extent, it being the only poorly played inning of the game."[ii]

Before and between the innings, gamblers circulated throughout the crowd, announcing betting odds changes as the game progressed. Once the fifth inning ended, the odds shifted sharply.

Here's how the *New York Herald* reported the scene the next day: "When the players first assembled the confidence in the Mutuals led to odds in the betting in their favor of one hundred to sixty; from that the betting went to eighty, ninety, and at last even, the excitement and interest increasing as the game progressed. It was soon clear that the Eckfords were outfielding [sic] their adversaries and equaling them at the bat; and when this became clear, the betting changed to odds in favor of the Eckfords, a large amount of greenbacks being invested by the friends of both parties."[iii]

There was no recovering from those eleven runs scored by the Eckfords. The game ended with an Eckfords' win of 23–11 over the Mutuals. This loss enraged the Mutuals' president. Once the game ended, he charged his team's catcher, William Wansley, with "willful and designed inattention" during the game.

Any doubts about what had transpired were soon dispelled once the Mutuals' shortstop, Thomas Devyr, made a written confession, explaining his role. Devyr wrote:

"Between eleven and twelve o'clock on the morning of the match, I was going toward the ferry, ready to go over to the ground, when I met Wansley, Duffy and another man in a wagon. Bill [Wansley] pulled up and asked where I was going. I told him I was going down toward the ferry and that I was going over to the ground in about an hour. He says, 'Do you want to make three hundred dollars?' I say I would like to do anything for that. He says, 'You can make it easy.' I asked how. [sic] He says, 'We are going to 'heave' this game, and will give you three hundred dollars if you like to stand with us. You need not do any of the work, [sic] I'll do all that myself and get all the blame.'[iv]

Wansley told Devyr that his and Duffy's participation in the scheme was merely to convince the gambler providing the money, that there were sufficient participants to ensure its success. The three received $100 before the game, of which Devyr got $30.[v]

All three players were banned from baseball. However, all three would eventually be reinstated to play. Devyr was reinstated after two years, and Duffy followed in 1868. Wansley was found to be the organizer and primary culprit; by 1870, his ban was also removed.[vi]

The banned umpire

Dick Higham made the record books as the only umpire banned from professional baseball. Prior to becoming an umpire in 1881, he began his first season as a player in 1870. During his ten-year playing career, Higham captained and/or managed several teams. He ended his professional playing days with a lifetime batting average of .307.

Higham became an umpire in 1881. It was alleged that while working in collusion with gamblers, he made incorrect calls against the Detroit Wolverines. After an investigation, the team's owner, William Thompson, fired Higham and banned him from the game for dishonesty. Higham denied all accusations.

(During the nineteenth century—a period of loosely organized baseball rules—no regular scheduling system existed for league umpires; occasionally even a player from another team would serve as a game's umpire.)

Honesty Prevails, July 22, 1873

Bob Ferguson had an impeccable reputation as a tough, honest, trustworthy, and talented player. Besides his position as a third baseman, he also held the office of president of the new National Association, and filled-in as a part-time umpire.

On July 22nd, 1873, Ferguson, along with his team, the Atlantics, played Baltimore in Brooklyn, losing that day by a score of 12–9. Immediately after the game, Ferguson convinced his team's loss that day and their previous 10–6 defeat on July 4th, were both fixed by gamblers.

He charged into the stands, going directly to the pool selling [gambling] area, and challenged the group of gamblers. Ferguson blasted the men with a variety of angry threats, then returned to the playing field, and confronted those players whom he suspected as being in cahoots with the gamblers.

The following day, the *Brooklyn Eagle* reported the confrontation by opining, "This is the first instance on record that either a player, a captain of a club nine or manager of any professional club, has had the moral courage to boldly and publicly denounce the gambling frauds which have brought such odium upon professional playing. Captain Ferguson certainly deserves great credit for thus boldly facing these knaves as he did." (Bob Ferguson, incidentally, became the only man in baseball history to simultaneously hold the positions of a player, manager, umpire, and league executive.)

Accusations and suspicions of baseball scandals had become commonplace throughout the 1873, 1874, and 1875 seasons. Therefore, it was no surprise when the 1875 season took its place in history as the most scandal ridden period of all, and become known as the real reason for the collapse of the National Association.

George Bechtel

The year 1876 brought no relief from gambling and game fixing, even though the new National League of Professional Baseball Clubs took over management. The first player disqualified under this new organization was George Bechtel in 1876; banned by Louisville for game fixing. He then discretely joined the New York Mutuals, and played in several games before the newly formed National League again banned his participation.

At the onset of the 1877 season, one of the major challenges for this new National League was to prove to the public, that member clubs were committed to eliminating gambling and crooked play. The public viewed this new league with skepticism, and rightfully so.

When the public realized the League was taking action against players such as Bechtel, confidence began to build. Many viewed these proceedings as a positive turning point in baseball's battle against crooked play.

Not unexpectedly, the League's first accusation of 1877 brought forth a report, on August 1st, of a scandal involving an attempted bribery dispute between a team's manager and an umpire. The investigation revealed the allegations to be one man's word against the other; no evidence of wrongdoing was found; no action taken.

Yet, within this hotbed era of betting, hard drinking, and corruption, it would have been unwise to assume that gambling and other forms of dishonesty would fade away. As the second year of the National League's existence was coming to a close, baseball's most notorious scandal of the nineteenth century was on the horizon.

The Louisville Grays Scandal

When it comes to uncovering game fixing and/or other forms of dishonesty within baseball circles, the information relating to such acts generally comes from an insider, or someone who has a grudge to settle. This was not the case involving the Louisville Grays.

The 'pennant fixing' lid was blown off by a single reporter who became suspicious of poor play and the collapse of one of, if not the best, team in the National League.

Here's the story

The 1877 Louisville Grays roster included some of the most talented baseball players in the League. Throughout the season, the Grays had lived up to expectations, and proven themselves to be a powerhouse team with an outstanding winning record.

By August 13, with a twenty-seven and thirteen record, they were in first place. In second place, trailing by three and a half games were the Boston Red Stockings.

On August 15, with just twenty games to play before season's end, the Grays left to play the first eight games of their season ending road series against Hartford (which was playing its games in Brooklyn, NY) and Boston.

When this series concluded, the Grays possessed a humiliating record of no wins, seven losses, and one tie game. *What went wrong?* The Grays appeared to suddenly collapse: The team's star pitcher, Jim Devlin, considered one of the best hurlers in the League, had lost his effectiveness.

Other players, including left fielder George Hall—the 1876 National League's home run king—made several fielding errors. Hall's plate appearances suffered even worse. To further compound their overall sloppy play, on their way back home, the Grays lost two of the four games they played against Cincinnati.

Boston, meanwhile, was enjoying a successful road trip to St. Louis and Chicago. Their win over Chicago on September 21 virtually clinched the league title, giving the Red Stockings a four game lead, with just five to play. The official pennant clinching game took place on the 30th of September.

Aware of rumors concerning gambling, the *Boston Globe* declared that "Boston has clinched the championship ... with no underhanded work ... never a hint at Boston's selling a game, as they have played so squarely as to give no one a chance to even think of crooked playing on their part."

By time the Grays returned home, they had suffered nine official defeats, and several losses to non-league clubs. Worst of all, they had not only lost the championship, they had also lost the confidence of the public.

Now that the pressure of the pennant chase was over, the Grays began to win. After a nine to six loss to Chicago on September 27, the team won all but one of its remaining games to clinch second place. And with thirty wins and twenty losses (not counting the Cincinnati games), the Grays finished the season two games behind Boston.

The Fix

John A. Haldeman, a sports reporter for the *Louisville Courier-Journal,* and also the son of part-owner and president of the Louisville Grays, was surprised by the unusual turn around—going from playing like a deplorable team during their quest to finish in first place—and once out of the pennant race, immediately returning to their winning ways.

Haldeman, perplexed by this sudden change in the quality of play by the Grays' stars, analyzed the data of each of those losses to Boston, and noticed a suspicious pattern: All of Boston's runs were scored in the final two innings of each game. Haldeman expanded his investigation to include tracking and comparing the productivity of select Grays' players against their earlier season's play; also in relation to other league players.

The more comparisons, the greater his speculation increased that something was amiss. The players with the most noticeable issues, that spoiled their team's chances for several victories, were the shortstop Bill Craver, pitcher Jim Devlin, outfielder George Hall, and the third baseman Al Nichols.

On October 18, ten days after regular season's play, the *Courier-Journal* published an article containing the following, "it had learned some 'interesting things' about the Grays which would make good reading in time and will not have to be looked at through spectacles to be made distinct and convincing."

Unbeknownst to the public, throughout the latter part of October, John Haldeman's findings had been discussed in a series of secret meetings with the Grays' directors. According to the *Courier-Journal*, which claimed much of the credit for uncovering the scandal, the paper's suspicions about specific players surfaced during mid season. However, it was the seven-game losing streak that translated those suspicions into certainty.

As for developing evidence against the players, various sources indicated that a few of the players, including Hall, Nichols, and Craver, showed up around town wearing expensive diamond pins and rings. However, those accusations went unconfirmed.

One of the more valid pieces of information came from the Grays' vice president, Charles E. Chase. He reported receiving two anonymous telegrams from Hoboken, New Jersey, during the losing streak. The first telegram implied that something dishonest was going on with the Louisville players, since gamblers were betting on the second-rate Hartford team. The second telegram predicted a Louisville loss the following day. The Grays lost that game because of sloppy play during critical situations.

Haldeman sensed a game fix; he filled his articles with well chosen inferences of what had taken place. The players, he suspected, got nervous, thinking Haldeman knew more than he actually did—the "empire" was crumbling. The Grays' board of directors also was feeling the newspaper's pressure that no "whitewash" would go unnoticed by the public.

Vice president Chase confronted both Devlin and Hall. Feeling the pressure, Hall was led to believe Devlin had confessed—so, he also confessed—telling Chase that he'd been doing wrong; but insisting he'd never thrown a league game. Hall asked Chase for leniency in return for a full and detailed confession. But Chase refused, implying that he'd learned all the details necessary from Devlin. Hall then gave a full confession, implicating Devlin and Nichols.

Devlin, confronted with Hall's confession, likewise told what he knew, and centered the blame on Nichols. As the story was pieced together, it turned out that Nichols knew a pool seller [gambler] named James McCloud. Through Nichols, McCloud paid both Devlin and Hall $100 to throw a game at Cincinnati, which they did. They next agreed to throw a nonleague game at Indianapolis, which the Grays lost 7–3.

But, the conspirators claimed, they did not receive any money for their "heave." Hall stated that he and Nichols had planned to throw another nonleague game against the Lowell, Massachusetts club; but, said he'd never been paid for that either.

On October 30, 1877, the directors of the Louisville Grays

expelled Bill Craver (shortstop), Jim Devlin (pitcher), George Hall (outfielder), and Al Nichols (third base). Hall, Devlin, and Nichols were banned for "selling games, conspiring to sell games, and tampering with players. Craver was expelled for disobedience of positive orders, general misconduct, and suspicious play, in violation of his contract and the rules of the league."

According to the *Courier-Journal,* none of the players admitted to throwing any of those crucial games during the seven-game losing streak at Boston and Hartford. However, the League banned all four for life.

The Louisville Grays' scandal became the first documented case of player corruption after the National League was founded. This scandal was also responsible for the disbanding of the Louisville franchise.

Gambling had been present in baseball well before the Louisville Grays scandal of 1877, and game fixing would continue long after that period—at least until 1919 and the famous "Black Sox" scandal.

Chapter 5

The 1919 Big Fix:
100 Years Later

"Say it ain't so, Joe, say it ain't so."

– Apocryphal tale that captured history

The 1919 "Black Sox" Scandal

This year will mark the one hundredth anniversary of the "Big Fix," Major League Baseball's most notorious and enduring scandal: The "heaving," or throwing, of the 1919 World Series. It is well known that gamblers had long been greasing the palms of disgruntled players in exchange for inside

tips on a game by game basis. But for a group of gamblers and ballplayers to team up, and form a conspiracy to manipulate the outcome of an entire World Series, was indeed a rare undertaking.

We know that the "fix" did happen—that appears undeniable—but who did exactly what, is anything but certain. What ultimately proved most scandalous about the crooked 1919 World Series was not merely the "fix" by the players, but the cover-up carried out by

A graphic run by various newspapers in 1920 after the Black Sox Scandal.

organized baseball, assisted by the gamblers themselves.[i]

There is the explosive and fragmentary rhetoric of a revealing word here and there, a missing or unreported detail, newly discovered facts, a secret exposed in a civil lawsuit. Little by little, the fascinating tale of the 1919 World Series scandal has continued to resurface, exposing more of the shocking truth that was buried beneath all the speculation and myths.

For example, forty-three years after the "fix," became public, a twenty-three-year-old Chicago White Sox office boy, Fred Krehbiel, discovered a book hidden in the basement of Comiskey Park. Harry Grabiner's journal contained, in partial form, a collection of documents, notations, and team salaries.

It also included a description of the events surrounding the initial investigation by Comiskey, of the fixing of the 1919 World Series, after it was unearthed in September, 1920. Grabiner was Charles Comiskey's longtime confidant, and White Sox's general manager from 1915–1945. This informative journal later became known as "Harry's Diary."

Excerpts from "Harry's Diary" were published by Bill Veeck and Ed Linn in their 1965 book, *The Hustler's Handbook*. Shedding further light on the Series "fix" was the 2013 discovery of another collection of missing "Black Sox" documents.

This unique find caused researchers and sports experts to reconsider the accuracy of what had been previously reported. Joining in the hot pursuit to recover allegedly stolen grand jury transcripts and documents, *Lelands.com*, a prominent New York sports memorabilia auction house, posted a $1 million bounty for "Shoeless" Joe Jackson's missing grand jury confession.

Gravest sin in the history of American sports

Much of what we have learned over the past decades is based upon bits and pieces of information, woven together to describe a confirmed conspiracy of corrupt, professional baseball players. Now, decades later, the pursuit to uncover the most significant pieces of evidence in the case has intensified. Even today, baseball authors, historians, and fans, are still interested in finding out, *what really happened?*

If you are a baseball fan, you have likely seen at least one, or both, of two movies: *Eight Men Out* and *Field of Dreams*. Or, perhaps you have thrown your heart and mind into the captivating stories told in

73

those huge numbers of articles and books written about the scandal. And yet, much remains a mystery as to what actually happened.

Well, if you think you know the real story of the Chicago White Sox throwing the 1919 World Series... think again!

The Rest of the Story

The late Paul Harvey, a radio and TV personality phenomenon for decades, was a master at connecting yesterday to the present and to tomorrow, in his highly popular segment, "The Rest of the Story." That is what this chapter is about.

Here we are, one century beyond that October 1919 "Black Sox" scandal. Yet, it is amazing that so many unanswered questions remain. Questions like: Exactly how was the "fix" organized? Which players truly participated? Why was the "fix" ignored, until almost a year later? Why weren't those players asking to stand trial alone be allowed to do so? What really happened to those "stolen" grand jury papers, and alleged confessions, that mysteriously disappeared before the trial got underway? Why was the kingpin gambler, Arnold Rothstein, never indicted? Why didn't Major League Baseball really investigate the conspiracy and alleged cover-up? *Perhaps the true answers will never be known.*

The heart of the scandal

At the heart of the "Black Sox" scandal is a longstanding and malicious connection between baseball and professional gamblers. As cited in Chapter 4, baseball had for some time, been living uneasily with the knowledge that bribes were being offered by gamblers, and some players were accepting them. A few actual case histories, such as the one involving the New York Mutuals (noted in Chapter 4), revealed that gamblers and ballplayers were in cahoots, as early as the mid-1800s.

Eliot Asinof's 1963 best-selling book, *Eight Men Out* (later made
into a 1988 movie by the same name) was written without
the author having access to grand jury statements, and other
important materials, including "Shoeless" Joe Jackson's alleged
confession. (Six months prior to the start of the "Black Sox" trial
on June 27, 1921, these documents were reported "stolen," and
would not reappear—with exception of "Shoeless" Joe Jackson's
alleged confession—until seventy years later. As for Jackson's
"confession," it suddenly reappeared in the briefcase of Comiskey's
attorney during Jackson's 1924 civil trial against the White Sox in
Milwaukee, Wisconsin.

Mystery Remains

What actually took place before, during, and after, all attempts to
hide the "fix" of the 1919 World Series will likely never be known.
Asinof's *Eight Men Out* should not be judged as the final accurate
account as to what really happened. Like a complex and secretive
course of action, no single person could possibly have all the facts
about what had taken place in the most enormous scandal in Major
League Baseball history.

To make this complicated story more riveting, the "Black Sox" eight
and their innocent teammates—clearly apprehensive by remnants
of shame and fear—chose to maintain their silence. Those who
knew the wide-ranging story, Ban Johnson, Charles Comiskey,
August Herrmann, and Alf Austrian, are all dead.

Few baseball stories possess the ability to continue to motivate
the public's interest as does this intriguing mystery. For example,
just Google the words, *1919 World Series "Black Sox" scandal,* and
don't be surprised to find around 107,000 results on this topic
alone. Therefore, with the demands to learn as much as possible
about this historical event, a huge number of historians, academics,
reporters, and authors, all gathering a hodge-podge of information

and materials, and formulating a variety of tales around their discoveries, have made for some interesting reading.

As the years pass, this story somehow continues to regain life. Newly discovered facts are bringing forth more clarity as to what actually took place; a previously unreported detail here, and/or a crucial secret exposed in a lawsuit there. Little by little, piece by piece, the unsavory, yet irresistible, story of the 1919 World Series scandal is brought back to life. *And, what a story it is!*

Background

Much of what we have learned about this scandal came from Eliot Asinof's *Eight Men Out*. However, it is important not to accept as correct, all that is described in the book. In other words, while getting the story correct in a number of places, he was not privy to enough of the facts to capture the true history of this deplorable event.

A fair amount of what he described in *Eight Men Out* was either inaccurate or incomplete. There is also contradiction. For example, I have never found evidence indicating that Buck Weaver, the White Sox third baseman, ever agreed to participate in throwing the Series. From day one until his death on January 3, 1956, Weaver always strongly denied ever agreeing to participate in the "fix".

However, in the first chapter of *Eight Men Out,* one paragraph infers the opposite: "There was, however, one incredible circumstance that would have a bearing on the outcome: eight members of the Chicago White Sox had agreed to throw the World Series."[ii] Another apparent contradiction appears on page 125, paragraph two: "There was no reason to pay Weaver. Though he had attended the pre-Series meetings, he had played baseball only to win."

Asinof had to rely, in large part, on newspaper articles and various other accounts. As result of timing, he did not have access to the "stolen" court papers and testimonial transcripts that had suddenly reappeared decades later. Therefore, important facts were either omitted, or altered, to best fit the story line of his book.

Also, his narratives occasionally failed to separate actual happenings from fiction. For example, his notes—archived in the Chicago History Museum—contain no record of interviews with Eddie Cicotte, Charles Comiskey, Hugh Fullerton, or Joe Jackson. Yet, the "thoughts" of each of these men were described in explicit detail; each appeared to have been written based on firsthand information.

Asinof also included the "thoughts" of the White Sox general manager, Harry Grabiner. Again, it appeared as though he had just finished interviewing him—a questionable "fact." Grabiner died in 1948, and Asinof's research got underway in 1960.

In addition, the author's use of fictional characters, within a supposedly nonfiction story, added questions about its historical value. I think it's safe to say, there was a fair amount of murkiness in this alleged "non-fiction" book.

The ground work

It is not my intention to make any attempt to retell those stories already covered in numerous other books such as Asinof's, Gene Carney's *Burying the Black Sox*, Charles Fountain's *The Betrayal*, and others. However, to make this chapter understandable, I need to retell a few noteworthy parts. Some of these provide more dimension to those facts I had not previously known. What better place to start than the headline that shockingly awoke our nation?

The *New York Evening World's* headline was outrageous when the newspaper hit the streets on December 15, 1919: "Is Big League Baseball Being Run for Gamblers, with Players in the Deal?" Those thirteen words would change the game of baseball forever. The author of this explosive article was no other than the highly respected sports reporter, Hugh Stuart Fullerton.

Back story:

Hugh Fullerton was a unique reporter. Before 1919 he had written over 100 freelance magazine articles, the majority of them for *American Magazine,* one of the largest and finest contemporary publications in the first quarter of the century. Fullerton was much more than a successful syndicated sportswriter.

To him, baseball was a sport in which the results made perfect sense. He was unshakable in his belief that he had developed a scientific system of predictive baseball statistics, capable of forecasting the outcome of games. He believed that the very essence of baseball lay in the certainty that he could predict individual games and season long results, by applying a quantitative or scientific system.[iii]

Prior to leaving on a late fall fishing trip, Fullerton had presented a number of his most critical concerns about the outcome of the 1919 World Series to Charles Comiskey and other Major League Baseball officials. Upon his return, Fullerton discovered that no action had been taken.

He insisted on a cleanup—not a whitewash. With a sense of outrage, Fullerton began to write a series of articles aimed at jolting the executive world of baseball into action. He exposed what every decent baseball writer knew, but never had the courage to write.[iv]

The headline article's impact

Many read Fullerton's article in stunned silence. Few ventured to accept the headline, although rumors had previously abounded that something was wrong. However, by reading the other newspapers such as the *Chicago Tribune,* Philadelphia's *North American,* and the *Chicago Herald,* there was not the slightest hint of any questionable behavior.

The news remained mostly positive. Weekly editions of *The Sporting News,* and the monthly publication, *Baseball Magazine,* provided interesting interviews and stories about popular baseball personalities.

Not a single publication, other than the *New York Evening World's* explosive article by Hugh Fullerton, dared to report on the real story. It started with the question, "Had the Chicago White Sox "heaved" the 1919 World Series to the Cincinnati Reds?"

Suspicions?

That's right… before the first ball was pitched, rumors had spread like wildfire, that gamblers had succeeded in corrupting the one sport which had been considered incorruptible.

In the days leading up to the start of the World Series, Hugh Fullerton had fears that the games were going to be fixed. The bulk of his suspicions came from the betting odds that were swinging heavily away from the highly favored White Sox. As the first game approached, the Reds were favored to win with the odds around eight-to-five.

Money talks… and Fullerton knew this. Not only could you look to the numbers, just listen to the noise on the street: "The Sox were going to throw the championship to Cincinnati," a story no other reporter would dare touch.

The conspiracy

I can only imagine what might have actually taken place that fateful morning, but it might have gone something like this.

Friday, September 19, 1919: As the sun was starting to rise on this cool morning in Boston, the Chicago White Sox's first baseman,

"Chick" Gandil, with his address book in hand, picked up his hotel room telephone and placed a local call to his longtime friend, Joseph "Sport" Sullivan; a well connected Boston gambler.

Within two hours, Sullivan passed through the lobby of Hotel Buckminster on Beacon Street. He took the elevator up to Gandil's room. Something was up, Sullivan thought. The two had known each other for eight years. It was the excitement in "Chick's" voice that caused Sullivan to sense something big! This had nothing to do with those tips that had helped with his betting on ball games when Gandil was with Washington. His tone projected something much more important.

Gandil opened his door, and greeted Sullivan with his normally rough, rube-like manner. No one else was in the room. Once the small talk ended, Gandil said he was in a rush; the team would be leaving shortly to head over to Fenway Park. In his abrupt and unpolished way, Gandil got down to business. He opened up, and started to talk about the upcoming World Series.

Suddenly, Sullivan sensed exactly where his friend was headed. The next words out of Gandil's mouth dropped like a bomb. Something that Sullivan had never contemplated, even in his wildest dreams... "I think we can put it in the bag!"

The plan's details were briefly discussed. Next, Gandil said he needed $80,000 in cash, to bring onboard a sufficient number of players to insure the Series would be lost by the highly favored White Sox.

As Sullivan got on the elevator, he must have acknowledged to himself that such a farfetched scheme was doable. It would be the biggest "fix" ever, in the history of baseball; or any sport for that matter.

Here was the chance for his largest payoff by far. As the elevator opened on the ground floor, Sullivan thought, "This can f---kin' be pulled off!"

The 1919 Chicago White Sox (Photo, National Baseball Library)

Advance Planning

Unbeknownst to Sullivan, over the past few months Gandil had been secretly approaching a few of the players to "test the waters," to see if they would go along with helping to throw the Series. Thanks to Charles Comiskey, the team's owner, the club was jam-packed with dissension. Players had suffered dramatic salary cuts and broken promises.

Gandil's timing and conditions to proceed were perfect. Cash payments, in advance, were the players' biggest issue. He brought Sullivan into the deal primarily because he did not know anyone else who had the resources to produce the $80,000 in cash that would be needed.

Two days after his talk with "Sport" Sullivan in Boston, on September 21st, a group of eight players secretly assembled, in "Chick" Gandil's room at the Ansonia Hotel, in New York City. As the informal meeting got underway, surprisingly, the tone within the room was, more on the lighthearted side, than serious. Players joked about paying bonuses to those who make the most errors. Another laughed about how he would plan to get hit on the head when a high fly slipped through his glove.

With the humor aside, Gandil got down to business. He made certain that the players understood what was involved from their prospective. He gave an update regarding his talk with "Sport" Sullivan. Naturally, the $80,000 payment was top priority on his list. He carefully emphasized that each player's share was to be paid in advance.

He said that details relating to how the games were to be 'heaved,' would be decided later by Sullivan and his financial backers. Two other things coming into play would be how Kid Gleason (manager) selected his pitchers—and how the gamblers would choose to manipulate the odds.

Sitting in the room were eight of baseball's best players; a few were idols to millions of fans. The group consisted of:

"Chick" Gandil, the "fix" originator and organizer. At thirty-one years old, he was acknowledged by many as one of the best first basemen in the American League; both for his play on the field and his outstanding work ethic.

In 1916, a Cleveland newspaper had described Gandil as "a most likeable player, and one of excellent habits." He had been in baseball for fourteen years. Playing first base, he was a solid .280 hitter. It was during his 1912 to 1915 stint with the Washington Senators that he became friends with "Sport" Sullivan. While game and player-related information was casually shared between the two, nothing illegal was noted. Gandil was sold to Cleveland in 1916, and in February 1917, he was sold to Chicago.

"Shoeless" Joe Jackson's biggest handicap was that he had minimal education and never learned to read or write. But he was widely recognized as the best natural hitter in baseball. In 1911, while playing for the Cleveland Naps (Indians), he made a major leap

to stardom. When the American League's season ended, Jackson had 233 hits, 45 doubles, 19 triples, and a .408 batting average. Although Jackson did not win the batting title (Detroit's Ty Cobb batted .420), he broke the Cleveland team's records for hits, average, and outfield assists.

Jackson's torrid hitting helped lift the Naps to a third-place finish. Ty Cobb paid tribute to Jackson at the season's end, "Joe is a grand ball player, and one who will get better and better. There is no denying that he is a better ball player his first year in the big league than anyone ever was."[v]

"Shoeless" Joe Jackson played for three Major League teams during his twelve-year career. He spent 1908–1909 playing for the Philadelphia Athletics, and the 1910 season with the minor league's New Orleans Pelicans, before joining the Cleveland Naps at the end of that season. Jackson remained in Cleveland through the first part of 1915. He played the remainder of the 1915 season through 1920 with the Chicago White Sox.

Charles "Swede" Risberg: In 1915, Risberg became a full-time utility player for the Tigers. He played in 175 games in 1915, and 185 in 1916, despite indifferent hitting performances. As a fielder, he spent time at first base, second base, shortstop, the outfield, and occasionally pitched. Risberg made his debut on April 11, 1917, with the White Sox. At that time, he was the youngest member of the Sox's team, a below-average hitter.

However. due to Risberg's superb defensive abilities, he won the full-time job at shortstop. Later in the season, Risberg went into a poor hitting slump. He only pinch-hit twice; both times when the Sox beat the New York Giants in the 1917 World Series. The next season, Risberg briefly left the White Sox for family reasons. He returned to the team for the pennant-winning 1919 season. In September, Risberg received good press in the *Atlanta Constitution*, which labeled him a "miracle man who had blossomed out as a wonder, after making four plays that were phenomenal."

George "Buck" Weaver was praised as the classiest third baseman in the game. He was as agile as a cat, defiant, and the only man Ty Cobb refused to bunt against. Initially a right-handed batter, Weaver learned to switch-hit, after a poor rookie season.

It was after this change at the plate that he became known as one of the American League's most resourceful players; twice leading the circuit in sacrifices. Weaver used his excellent fielding range to reach balls that escaped most of his peers. He was also known as a steady .300 hitter.

Oscar "Happy" Felsch, known for his easygoing nature and wonderful smile made his family's nickname, "Happy," a perfect fit. Newspapers adopted the nickname as early as 1912. On August 8, 1914, the White Sox acquired Felsch for $12,000, plus an infielder and an outfielder for their organization.

The 1915 season developed into an eventful one for the White Sox's rookie center fielder. Felsch made his major league debut on April 14, against St. Louis, with a single and a stolen base. By the end of the 1916 season, Felsch and his teammates had advanced to second place, and finished only two games behind the first place Boston Red Sox.

Eddie Cicotte made his major-league debut with Detroit on September 3, 1905. The Boston Red Sox purchased Cicotte's contract for $2,500 at the end of the 1907 season. He was believed to be the first major league pitcher to master the knuckleball. Cicotte once estimated that seventy-five percent of the pitches he threw were knuckleballs.

The rest of the time this right-hander relied on a fadeaway, slider, screwball, spitter, emery ball, shine ball, and a pitch he called the "sailor," a rising fastball that would sail in much the same manner as a flat stone skimming over water.

On July 22, 1907, the Red Sox sold Cicotte's contract to the Chicago White Sox. In 1913 Cicotte enjoyed his first standout season in the major leagues, posting an eighteen win, eleven loss record to go along with a 1.58 ERA; second best in the American League. In 1917, Cicotte moved into the pitchers' starting rotation, and enjoyed the best season of his career. The White Sox captured their first pennant in eleven seasons.

During 1919 Cicotte regained his 1917 form, pitching the White Sox to their second pennant in three years. Once again, he led the American League in victories (29), and innings pitched (306–2/3, tied with Jim Shaw). His twenty-nine-and-seven record was good enough to lead the league in winning percentage (.806), and his 1.82 ERA, ranked second.

Claude "Lefty" Williams was considered one of the most promising left-handers in baseball. He recorded back-to-back twenty-win seasons with the White Sox in 1919 and '20. He was being groomed to replace Eddie Cicotte as the team's pitching ace.

Apparently, none of the eight of these men gave any thought to the consequences they would later incur. However, the group did use some caution when they left Gandil's room; they left one by one to avoid arousing suspicion.

The Deal

When Cicotte exited, he headed to the Ansonia's lobby. Perhaps by coincidence, Cicotte ran into Bill "Sleepy Bill" Burns, a former third-rate pitcher with the Detroit Tigers, and now a well-connected gambler. As competing pitchers on rival teams, the two had chewed the fat on various occasions. After a quick Hello, Burns asked, "Was there a plan to 'fix' the Series?" Cicotte replied there was always that kind of talk and rumors going around.

However, Cicotte's stammering response indicated something was up. This was all Burns needed. He began to question Cicotte for details. Shortly thereafter, Burns heard what he suspected. There was a plan, and money was the issue. Burns begged Cicotte to hold up on any decision, until he could gather resources wealthy enough to handle such a big undertaking.

Burns immediately went to work. He summonsed Billy Maharg, a mediocre Philadelphia gambler, to hop a train to New York and meet him at the Ansonia Hotel. A deal this big required major financing. The following morning, Burns and Maharg met Cicotte in the hotel's lobby. However, this time Cicotte was not alone; Gandil was with him.

As all expected, money was the biggest issue. Burns asked how much the players needed. Gandil—now in control of the talks—told Burns they would throw the Series for $100,000. As with "Sports" Sullivan, Burns and Maharg did not have that kind of dough, so they would have to find a moneyman capable of fronting that kind of cash.

Gandil had initially approached "Shoeless" Joe Jackson earlier in September, and offered him $10,000; which was refused. Once the offer was increased to $20,000, "Shoeless" Joe agreed to participate. Jackson's real reason for joining the game fixing conspiracy will never become known.

Feeding Frenzy

Between Burns and Maharg, neither was able to raise anywhere near the money needed in Philadelphia. So, they took a trip to New York to meet the most notorious, well-heeled gambler, and moneymaking genius, Arnold Rothstein. Some gamblers referred to Rothstein as the "Big Bankroll."

Rothstein, sensing the two men would exploit whatever opportunity given them, moved away from Burns and Maharg, and made arrangements to deal with his old friend, "Sports" Sullivan. Rothstein sent one of his partners, Nat Evans, to join Sullivan at a meeting on September 29, to discuss the potential "fix" with Gandil and other unnamed players.

Gandil again demanded $80,000 in cash before the Series began, which was now only two days away. Evans relayed Gandil's demands to Rothstein, who wired $40,000 in cash to begin the process, and also sent another forty grand to be kept in a hotel safe, and only to be distributed after the Series was successfully fixed.

The initial $40,000 was given to Sullivan, who secretly revealed his greed; he gave Gandil only $10,000. He used the remaining $30,000 to place personal bets in an attempt to capitalize on Rothstein's money. Gandil didn't take kindly to what was taking place; he viewed this shortfall as a double-cross. He'd already promised Cicotte $10,000 to throw the first game. If that didn't happen, then the entire deal was off.

The players, who expected their cash payoffs in advance, reluctantly agreed to go ahead with the "fix". The plan was for Cicotte to hit the leadoff batter in the first game to signal that the "fix" was on. The gamblers had no interest in the order in which the games were lost—as long as the Sox came out the loser. That evening, Cicotte received his $10,000 in cash. The bills were left under his pillow, in his hotel room.

Tuesday, September 31:

The lobby of Cincinnati's Hotel Sinton—where the Sox were to stay—was filled with a throng of fans, sports reporters, as well as a sizable contingent of gamblers, including Bill "Sleepy Bill" Burns.

Moving almost unnoticed, behind the throng of Chicago players as they headed towards the check in desk, was another gambler, Abe Attell. The "Little Champ," as he was known, was there to assure the players that he had Arnold Rothstein's $100,000, but was told not to give it to them all at once; the payments were to be made in

$20,000 increments after each game they lost. (Attell would later meet in secret with seven of the "fix" ballplayers in Cicotte's room; Joe Jackson was missing.)

Court testimony would later suggest that Gandil and his gambling cohorts may have cut multiple deals with different syndicates. "They not only sold [the Series]," Abe Attell later claimed, "but they sold it wherever they could get a buck."

As "Sleepy Bill" Burns moved about the lobby, he met up with an old acquaintance, Hugh Fullerton, the sports reporter. The two struck up a conversation about the upcoming Series. Burns, speaking in a knowledgeable tone, offered Fullerton a tip, "The Reds are already in."

Fullerton found this comment disturbing. The rumors and predictions being spread around by various gamblers, in what initially was a "secret" to be shared only by a few, was now open knowledge; at least in the gambling circles.

Whistle-blower

That evening—the night before game one of the 1919 World Series started—Hugh Fullerton wired an article to all of his forty syndicated newspapers. Its headliner title read: **"ADVISE ALL NOT TO BET ON THIS SERIES. UGLY RUMORS AFLOAT."**

Despite all the caution used in wording his article, only two newspapers saw fit to publish this earth-shattering warning. From that point on, Hugh Fullerton was labeled a whistle-blower.

Wednesday, October 1:

By the time the ballplayers came downstairs for breakfast, the lobby was buzzing with action. Word on the street indicated betting was heavy as people—almost in a panic mode—were busy searching for places where they could get their hands on betting money. Loaded with watches, jewelry, tools, and clothing; everything that could be converted into cash was taken in—the pawn shops were packed.

Hugh Fullerton saw gamblers in the Sinton lobby, waving $1,000 bills in the air; a sight he had never before witnessed. As the suspected Sox players moved throughout the hotel, they showed no signs of concern. It was as if their betrayal was nothing new.

The evening prior, Charles Comiskey, the Chicago White Sox's owner, had a restless night. He also had heard the unsettling rumors. While he would later say that he didn't believe them for a second, he still had a restless night. After breakfast, Comiskey left the hotel for the ball park, attributing his poor night's sleep to pregame nerves.

Redland Field

Shortly after arrival at Redland Field, the players put on their uniforms and headed out for batting practice. During practice "Shoeless" Joe Jackson could not free himself of the pressures of the "fix." Later, he sat sullen and apart [from the other players], waiting for Kid Gleason [manager] to spot him. He told Gleason that he did not feel good, and didn't want to play. "You can tell the boss [Comiskey] too!" Gleason responded, "You'll play, Jackson. You'll play!" It was not a prediction; it was a threat.[vi]

Did Jackson actually make that statement?

Gene Carney's 2006 book, *Burying the Black Sox*, cites that there is no evidence of any pre-Series communication between Jackson and his team. This account of what took place only came from Jackson; there was no other validation.[vii]

The earliest known version of Jackson's claim is documented in *The Chicago White Sox Sport* newsletter, June 1951, in a team history article by John Carmichael. Joe Jackson is quoted as saying, "I went to Mr. Comiskey three weeks before the Series. I asked him to pull the team out; told him what I heard. He laughed and said, 'We got

100 men on guard... nothing could be pulled.'[viii]

Games On

Game One: Prior to the game getting underway, Cincinnati's Redland Field ballpark was overflowing its 30,000-seat capacity. Excited Chicago fans were energized and confident of victory as the Sox's star pitcher, Eddie Cicotte, took to the mound. As agreed with his gambling partners, he hit the first batter up on his second pitch. *The "fix" was on.*

In keeping with the plan to lose the first game, Cicotte, who went twenty-nine and seven in the regular season, surprised the fans— but not the gamblers—by giving up five runs in the fourth inning. Reds' pitcher, Dutch Reuther, threw a six-hitter; the Reds won, nine to one.

The Gamblers' Word

Gandil and his cohorts would soon learn that their $20,000 payoff was delayed. The ballplayers had initially said they weren't going to throw games without getting their money. Burns told Gandil they shouldn't worry. In the gambling world, things like this happen. The cash goes out on bets; it takes time to rake it in. He felt sure they'd get their money tomorrow.[ix]

That evening, Charles Comiskey was on edge. There were too many reports, especially one coming from the so-called horse's mouth. He was referring to a visit to his hotel room from Monte Tennes, a prominent Chicago gambler and sportsman. Tennes said he'd heard enough to bet a big chunk against Comiskey's ball club.

Once Tennes left the room, Comiskey summoned the team's manager, Kid Gleason, to his room. Gleason also hesitantly told what he had heard, and about a number of telegrams he had received from unknown gamblers, warning him that the Series was being fixed. "How do you like that!" he cried. "I don't even know these guys!" Comiskey was not interested in Gleason's telegrams; he had several of his own.[x]

At approximately 2:30 a.m., Comiskey, unable to sleep, woke up Ban Johnson, President of the American League and John Heydler, the President of the National League. The three met in Johnson's room at close to 3:00 a.m. The matter was briefly discussed. Comiskey was adamant in his belief that something terrible was going on. He admitted he had no proof.

Heydler insisted: "You can't fix a World Series, Commy!" Johnson's hatred of Comiskey would critically plague the investigation of the Series scandal, and alter its history. Comiskey nodded his appreciation to John Heydler, swallowed his shattered pride, and left the room. He was through for the night.[xi]

October 2nd, Game Two: The first thing "Chick" Gandil did that morning after leaving his room was to meet with the gamblers, and demand the payoff money. Here again, another stall. The $20,000 had not arrived. After much back-and-forth, Gandil was receptive to an offer that a $120,000 oil lease be put up as collateral.

Another glory day for the enthralled Redland fans and the fixers; the Reds won the game, four runs to two. The game was sealed when Larry Kopf hit a two-run triple in the fourth inning.

After the game, Gandil was expecting $40,000, to be split among the players. Abe Attell reneged again; he tossed only $10,000 on the bed for Burns to deliver to Gandil. "A double-cross!" Gandil shouted. Again, Burns assured Gandil that it was only a delay. They would be paid in full. Gandil said he would think about it, and took the money. He was in a rush to meet up with the team to catch the 11:00 p.m. sleeper train back to Chicago.

On the morning of game three, because the players hadn't received the money due them, the gamblers were nervous. What were the Sox players going to do; play to lose or win? When Burns contacted

"Chick" Gandil at the Warner Hotel, he was told that the boys had talked it over, and that it would go exactly like the first two games. When Burns told Attell the plan, Attell was skeptical.

However, Burns believed what Gandil had told him. Together, he and his partner, Billy Maharg, scraped together every dollar they could get their hands on, and put their big pot on the Sox to lose game number three.

The two men would later learn that "Chick" Gandil had lied. No discussion had taken place. The players had no intention of letting the third game go exactly like the first two. Their anger at the failure to receive payments as promised, was enough to preclude any further discussion. The truth was, nobody knew how the third game would go.[xii]

October 3rd, Game Three: Dickey Kerr, an up-and-coming rookie for the White Sox, drew the pitching start. Apparently untouched by the scandal, the tough lefthander refused to roll over and threw a three-hit, three runs to none, winner. Chicago was back in the race.

With that Sox win, Burns and Maharg lost everything. Their World Series came to an abrupt end; they left town.

October 4th, Game Four/October 6th Game Five: The inspired Reds, unaware that a "fix" was on, pitched back-to-back shutouts in games four and five, on the arms of Jimmy Ring and Hod Eller.

(In any other year, the World Series would have ended at this point; however 1919 was different. Due to the intense postwar interest, the Commissioner of Baseball had decided to extend this Fall Classic to a best of nine affair.)

By the time the series returned to Redland Field, the Reds had won four games, but with that year's new format, they needed one more win. The gamblers still hadn't paid the promised payoff money, so the "Black Sox," as they came to be known, went all out in both the October 7, game six, and game seven, October 8, and won both.

"Sports" Sullivan, surprised at the reenergized Sox team, found out that the "fix" deal was off. Gandil, and his seven other players, had been jerked around by Attell and his two flunkies. Sullivan panicked, in fear of what Rothstein would do if the Sox came back and won the Series.

He picked up the phone and started calling colleagues in Boston; Sullivan managed to raise twenty grand before noon. He told Gandil what he had learned about the deceitful way that Attell had operated, and to prove his good faith, he would wire $20,000 immediately. Sullivan also reminded Gandil of the money left in the hotel safe; another $40,000. Gandil agreed that if the $20,000 was received immediately, the players would likely reactivate the "fix". He reminded Sullivan that an additional $20,000 would be due before the eighth game. Sullivan quickly agreed.

Those two Chicago wins had reduced the Reds lead to only one game. Yet, the Reds were still favored to win the championship. However, Arnold Rothstein, unnerved by those two consecutive Sox wins, was taking no chances. He called "Sports" Sullivan, and arranged to meet.

The highlights of Rothstein's comments included the following: He suggested to Sullivan to see to it that the Series ends with the next game. He did not think it was wise that the Series be allowed to go to the ninth game. In short, he hoped to see it end quickly, in the first inning, if such a thing was possible.[xiii]

Sullivan knew that Rothstein meant business. Money was not the answer—it was too late. Sullivan hired a guy he knew in Chicago who was a "persuasion" expert. This man made contact with Lefty Williams, the upcoming game's scheduled pitcher. While no one knows exactly what transpired, Williams got the message. If he wanted to stay healthy, and keep his wife healthy, he would lose the eighth game—and lose it in the first inning.

As sportswriter Hugh Fullerton entered the ballpark for game eight, he was approached by a gambler with whom he was acquainted. The gambler told him to bet on Cincinnati. "It will be the biggest first inning you ever saw!"[xiv]

October 9th, Game Eight: Cincinnati dominated the final outing "with a little help" from their crooked rivals, in a ten-to-five romp; four runs were scored in the first inning. When the game ended, the Reds had won their first World Series Championship, in their first appearance.

Unfortunately, the victory would be bittersweet. The scandal would be confirmed a year later.

Busted!

Hugh Fullerton did what no other reporter had the guts to do. He reported on the 1919 World Series scandal. Fullerton also put pressure on the MLB Commissioner, and Comiskey, to investigate the claims, clear out the fog, and take action against those involved, if found guilty.

Up to this point, the corruption rumors were widespread, detailed, and were being talked about around the country. However, when Fullerton stepped up to the plate and began to analyze and question specific plays by certain players, he became convinced something was amiss.

With evidence in hand, he was able to gain the attention of MLB's executives and the legal authorities. Initially, it seemed everyone believed baseball was too large and pure to dive into gambling and scandal.[xvi] Fullerton also recalled for *The Sporting News*, how he first heard of the "fix," and what he did about it.[xvii]

Power of the Press

The media generally worked to unravel the truth, and provide the public with the correct information. During the months preceding the World Series, Hugh Fullerton provided information to the people by applying firm pressure onto those involved. He stunned the baseball world with his article titled, "Is Big League Baseball Being Run for Gamblers, with Players in the Deal?"

> *"Professional baseball has reached a crisis. The major leagues, both owners and players are on trial. Charges of crookedness among the owners, accusations of cheating, of tampering with each other's teams, with attempting to syndicate and control baseball, are bandied about openly. Charges that gamblers have succeeded in bribing ballplayers, that games have been bought and sold, that players are in the pay of professional gamblers and that even the World Series was tampered with are made without attempt at refutation by the men who have their fortunes invested in baseball… Some are for keeping silent and "allowing it to blow over." The time has come for straight talk. How can club owners expect writers, editors and fans to have any faith in them or their game if they make no effort to clean up the scandal?*[xviii]

Rebuttal was quick and scathing

The very next morning, after the above article was published, the *New York World* ran an article quoting Charles Comiskey, the Chicago White Sox owner:

> *"I can say that we have discovered nothing to indicate that the team double-crossed me or the public last fall. Do not get the impression we have quit investigating. I am still working on the affair, and will go the limit to get any evidence to support the truth of these charges. And if I land the goods on any of my players I will see to it that there is no place in organized baseball for them. There will be no whitewashing or compromising with crooks, but as yet not one bit of reliable evidence has turned up."*

Despite [Comiskey's] "claims to the contrary, evidence would later show that Comiskey had been tipped off about a possible "fix" early in the series, and may have attempted to bury the story to protect his business interests."[xix]

Attacks on Hugh Fullerton were widespread and cutting: *Baseball Magazine, Spalding Official Baseball Guide,* and others joined in.

Play Monitoring

Prior to the start of the Series, both Hugh Fullerton and former pitching great, Christy Mathewson, became concerned about the number of rumors they were hearing about a Series "fix". Neither believed the reports were true. Yet, the two men formed an alliance, and agreed that while working in the press box, they would circle any suspicious plays on their individual scorecards for later discussion.

Fullerton would later say that in the eight games, he and Mathewson marked just seven plays as "suspicious." Any one of those plays could be explained on the theory that the mistakes were honestly made, as well as on the theory of dishonesty. Plainly, the outsider cannot tell to a certainty.[xv]

Hugh Fullerton died on December 27, 1945 in Dunedin, Florida. He was posthumously awarded the J. G. Taylor Spink Award by the National Baseball Hall of Fame in 1964. The award honors a baseball writer (or writers) "for meritorious contributions to baseball writing," and is presented during Hall of Fame weekend by the Baseball Writers' Association of America.

Hugh Fullerton wrote many articles, but none more courageous than the one that led to the exposure of the 1919 World Series scandal.

The Grand Jury

Fullerton's hard-hitting articles about the suspected "fix" of the

1919 World Series caught the attention of a grand jury, initially convened to investigate the possibility that gamblers had rigged a regular season game on August 31, 1920, between the Chicago Cubs and Philadelphia Phillies. After reading some of what Fullerton had written, the grand jury quickly shifted their focus to the 1919 World Series.

On Monday, September 27, 1920, the *Philadelphia North American* published a story about gambler Bill Maharg's interview with reporter Jimmy Isaminger. The story startled millions of readers: "The Most Gigantic Sporting Swindle in the History of America." Maharg had related his own account of the "fix". *The cat was now out of the bag!*

Say it ain't so, Joe...

One of the most famous quotes in sports history is linked to September 28, 1920. On that day, according to Chicago's *Herald and Examiner*, as "Shoeless" Joe Jackson left the courthouse, after giving testimony to the grand jury, a heartbroken young boy went up to him and begged, "It ain't so, Joe, is it?" Jackson allegedly replied "Yes, kid, I'm afraid it is." As years passed, by 1940, this famous quote morphed into "Say it ain't so, Joe!" in rewritten accounts of the incident. (Jackson always denied any such thing was said by a kid, or anyone else, that day. In addition, there is no court record of Jackson admitting he was involved in fixing the game— and, publicly, he always denied it. Also, no eyewitness accounts corroborated either version of the quote. It is believed a reporter likely made up this story.)[xx]

Eddie Cicotte weeps

On September 29, Eddie Cicotte testified in front of the grand jury. He testified for two hours and eleven minutes, and sobbed bitterly through much of that time. He told of the details of the "fix," and how he received $10,000 the night before the first game. Cicotte also named the eight players, including himself, and the four gamblers that he knew were involved.

Upon hearing the news about Cicotte's confession, "Shoeless" Joe Jackson panicked, went to the courthouse that same afternoon, and told his story under oath.

Indicted

On October 22, 1920, the grand jury returned nine counts of conspiracy indictments against eight of the Chicago White Sox—now dubbed the "Black Sox"—players, and five gamblers. The following Chicago White Sox players were named in the indictments:

- Arnold "Chick" Gandil, first base
- Eddie Cicotte, pitcher
- Oscar "Happy" Felsch, center field
- "Shoeless" Joe Jackson, right field
- Fred McMullin, utility infielder
- Swede Risberg, shortstop
- Buck Weaver, third base

The gamblers indicted included Bill "Sleepy Bill" Burns, Joseph "Sport" Sullivan, and Abe Attell. Burns testified as a prosecution witness; it is not known if he was sent to prison. Sullivan and Attell would take a quick vacation out of the country. Arnold Rothstein was not indicted, became a government witness, and testified before the grand jury. He never suffered any of the consequences.

The above were accused of pulling off, what would go down as the greatest scandal in the history of sports; the 1919 "Black Sox" scandal. The country's fans were in shock; some even predicted end of the game.

A 1920 editorial in *The Nation* said, "We do not trust cashiers half as much, or diplomats, or policemen, or physicians, as we trust an outfielder or a shortstop, or as much as America trusted 'Shoeless' Joe Jackson and Oscar 'Happy' Felsch, both outfielders, or Swede Risberg, the shortstop—three of the eight Black Sox who conspired to throw the Series. To think and write otherwise, despite mounting evidence, was unthinkable and almost unprintable in America in 1919. Yet, Fullerton had the guts to write about a subject most American journalists, especially sportswriters, ignored; gambling."

The Trial

On June 27, 1921, the criminal trial of the eight Chicago White Sox players got underway. Among those in the overcrowded courtroom were many Chicago youngsters, fighting their way inside to feed on the sight of their heroes, in this bizarre setting. Nobody seemed to care that the gamblers were absent.

The defense opened with a motion to quash the trial, claiming that the indictments were illegal under Illinois law. A week later, on July 5, Judge Friend denied the defense's motion.[xxi]

On July 15, the final four of eight jurors were sworn in. The trial's opening remarks by the prosecutor, George Gorman, got underway on Monday, July 18.

Gorman described the 1919 Series "fix" as a chaotic chess game between gamblers and players: "The gamblers and ball players started double-crossing each other until neither side knew what the other intended to do."

The most startling occurrance took place immediately after all the State's star witnesses had completed their testimonies. State prosecutor Gorman, made a blockbuster announcement when he notified the Court that the original copies of the defendant's signed confessions and immunity waivers had disappeared. He explained that he had never seen the actual papers. They had been stolen before he had taken office; he did not know where they were, or what had happened to them. Gorman's response to the Judge's persistent questions was, "Ask Arnold Rothstein, maybe he knows!"[xxii]

While the eight players were ridiculed in the media for "selling out baseball," they coasted through their trial. All of the documents relating to their grand jury testimonies and confessions had vanished, sometime prior to July 23, 1921, under mysterious circumstances.

Many suspected that Comiskey and gambling kingpin, Rothstein, had arranged for the documents to be stolen, as part of a cover up. (Based on testimony presented during Jackson's 1924 civil trial, this assumption was incorrect.) The disappearance of those critical documents had a powerful impact. The prosecution's case was lost at the very moment of that announcement.

Not Guilty, but…

On August 2, 1921, the jury deliberated for less than three hours. The "Black Sox" eight were found 'not guilty' on all counts. However, the ballplayers' vindication celebration would not last long. Only one day after the acquittal, Commissioner of Baseball, Kenesaw Mountain Landis, decreed that all eight players were permanently banned from organized baseball.

"Regardless of the verdict of juries," Landis wrote, "no player who throws a ballgame, no player that undertakes or promises to throw a ballgame, no player that sits in conference with a bunch of crooked players and gamblers where the ways and means of throwing a game are discussed and does not promptly tell his club about it, will ever play professional baseball."[xxiii]

Cover-up?

As the years moved forward, all types of "cover-up" theories have evolved. For example, author Gene Carney, in his well researched book, *Burying the Black Sox*, talked of two cover-ups. "The first has to do with the Big Fix; for more than eleven months, the American public was kept in the dark about the throwing of the 1919 World Series."

When reading books such as *Eight Men Out*, a great deal of blame for the cover-up was placed at the feet of Charles Comiskey, owner of the Chicago White Sox. However, just as it would have been impossible for a player to single-handedly throw a World Series; it would have been beyond Comiskey's ability to execute the cover-up without help.

In his 1990 book, *1919: America's Loss of Innocence*, Eliot Asinof talked about the cover-up: "But mostly the secrecy was maintained by the power of the owners themselves. Whatever they knew, or suspected, they concealed, terrified at losing the public faith in the game. At all costs, any suspicious incidents would be buried." Asinof continued with his observation: "The cover-up was far better organized than the 'fix' itself. The baseball establishment had years of experience to fall back on."

Asinof also reflected on what Comiskey did not do when he learned the "fix" was in for certain. He went to Heydler [President of the National League]. He apparently did not see fit to walk into his own locker room, shut the doors to all outsiders, and take the bull by the horns. He did nothing, but cover his rear.[xxiv]

As word of the "fix" went into high gear, more and more people began to take note of possible cover-up rumors. Hugh Fullerton said that he went to Comiskey on the morning of game one, and told Comiskey what he had heard about an anticipated "fix" from two "big shot" Chicago gamblers. Comiskey said he had already heard about it. Fullerton said, "Commy was furious because Ban Johnson was doing nothing about it. Comiskey said Johnson knew about it, too—before game one."

Fullerton next went to Pittsburgh Pirates owner, Barney Dreyfuss. "I lost my temper and raised Cain with him and with the entire baseball set-up, calling them a bunch of whitewashing bastards who were letting a bunch of crooks get away with it because they were afraid of losing money."[xxv]

The strange trial of "Shoeless" Joe Jackson

In 1923, Jackson hired a Milwaukee based attorney, Ray Cannon, to represent him in a lawsuit against the Chicago White Sox for back pay he believed was owed to him after his acquittal. Jackson was convinced that Harry Grabiner, Comiskey's assistant, had taken advantage of his illiteracy in obtaining his signature on a contract that included the much hated "reserve clause," which effectively allowed teams to control their players in perpetuity.

In 1924, Jackson filed a civil court claim in Milwaukee. During the trial, Jackson's 1920 "confession" to the Chicago grand jury—which had mysteriously disappeared at the onset of the 1921 trial—resurfaced, in the possession of Comiskey's attorney. It was used by the Comiskey team as a legal weapon against Jackson.

However, the jury sided with Jackson, and awarded him more than $16,000 in back pay. The jury also believed Jackson was not involved in the 1919 World Series "fix".

Unfortunately for Jackson, the presiding judge overruled the jury, and set aside the verdict, claiming that his decision was based on Jackson's testimony at the trial, which was contradicted by his 1920 grand jury testimony. (The case was eventually settled out of court for an undisclosed amount.)

In 1989, the "confession" reappeared at the Chicago Historical Society, in an exhibition about the 1919 World Series scandal. Jackson's testimony was both conflicting and compelling.

Missing Documents

In December 2007, a collection of documents, most related to the Black Sox scandal, plus all of those originating in the offices of the lawyers for Charles Comiskey, was purchased at auction by the Chicago History Museum for nearly $100,000.

Among the papers were reports from the detectives whom Comiskey hired through his lawyer, Alfred S. Austrian. A letter summarizing their findings, dated May 11, 1920, from J. R. Hunter, of Hunter's Secret Service of Illinois, was among the exhibits in the separate 1924 trial, when Joe Jackson sued the White Sox for breach of contract. But the rest of the documents, twenty-eight in all, have probably never been seen for close to ninety years, and they had never before been made public.[xvi]

100th anniversary

This year will mark one century since this disdainful incident took place. Baseball authors, historians, and fans are still searching to find out what really happened. For example, ninety-six years later (August 2015), supporters of legendary baseball star "Shoeless" Joe Jackson lost in their attempt to get Major League Baseball Commissioner, Rob Manfred, to reconsider the lifetime ban that cost the turn of the century baseball great a place in the Hall of Fame. Manfred said his team researched the matter, and he found no reason to reverse rulings by his predecessors, that Jackson's gambling should bar him from Cooperstown. "I agree with that determination and conclude that it would not be appropriate for me to reopen this matter," Manfred wrote to the officials at the Joe

Jackson Museum in Greenville, S.C.[xxvii]

Mystery Remains

It would not be until decades later that what took place on the field and in the courtroom, and the involvement of gamblers, would start to emerge. Much of what had been written during those earlier days revolved around supposition, incomplete, and inaccurate stories.

Today, a number of select court documents from the Chicago Black Sox Trial of 1921 are available for viewing on the internet at *http://famous-trials.com/legacyftrials/blacksox/courtdox.html*.

Those documents include:

- Joe Jackson's Statement ("Confession") Before the Grand Jury (September 28, 1920)

- Statement of Claude "Lefty" Williams (September, 1920)

- Petition of George "Buck" Weaver & Joe Jackson (arguing their innocence) (February 1921)

- People vs Edward Cicotte, et al: Bill of Particulars (February, 1921)

- Trial Testimony (July, 1921)

The "Black Sox" scandal dramatically altered organized Baseball's position towards corruption. This revision brought about some much needed change in the ways baseball policed its leagues and players. Those in charge discovered the key to the game's survival was constant vigilance against corruption: Any suspicion investigated, any scandal pursued, and any dishonest players expelled from baseball.

The Aftermath

The dealings that led up to the 1919 World Series scandal will continue to fade into the history of baseball. However, the memory of this scandal will live forever.

Today, when I talk with others about the "Black Sox" scandal, it is not uncommon for the conversation to shift to two of the eight players actually charged: Buck Weaver and "Shoeless" Joe Jackson.

Buck Weaver devoted most of his life after the expulsion, attempting to clear his name. He made numerous appeals to Commissioner Landis for reinstatement, but all were denied.

To make a living, while residing in Chicago, Weaver tried his hand at operating two retail establishments, a drugstore, and later, a sandwich shop; both failed. He next took a job as a painter for the City of Chicago. From there, the last job he would hold was as a pari-mutual clerk for Chicago's Sportsman's Park. Buck Weaver suffered a fatal heart attack on January 3, 1956.

As for Weaver's role in the "fix," I found no evidence that supports the allegation that he played an active part in throwing the Series. Furthermore, he received no money for his involvement. The major sin that Buck Weaver committed was allegedly attending two fix-related meetings; he was well aware of what was coming down. His failure to report this information to baseball officials was his downfall.

According to an article in *The Wall Street Journal,* "(Baseball Commissioner) Landis later told a newspaper interviewer that, at a meeting in his office after he had rendered his decision, Weaver confessed that he attended two sessions with the fixers."[xviii]

"Shoeless" Joe Jackson has reached legendary status within the baseball world. His claim to fame is that he holds baseball's third-best all-time career batting (.356) average, behind Ty Cobb and Rogers Hornsby. Jackson's natural hitting abilities were praised by both Ty Cobb and Babe Ruth. In 1998, Ted Williams lobbied—unsuccessfully—for Jackson to be voted into the Hall of Fame.

Jackson is often depicted as a victim of organized baseball. Many believe that he was misled, as result of his poor education and inability to read and write, especially when it came to understanding important papers and contracts. As with Weaver, Jackson also maintained his innocence, and stood by his playing record in the Series.

Back in Greenville, Jackson operated a restaurant and a liquor store for several years, and also taught baseball to local youngsters. In September, 1951, Cleveland Indians' fans honored Jackson by voting him into the team's Hall of Fame. On December 5, 1951, two weeks prior to his scheduled appearance on Ed Sullivan's "Toast of the Town" show, Jackson, age 63, suffered a heart attack and died at home.

Jackson admitted to receiving $5,000 after the Series ended. He later said that he had tried, unsuccessfully, to both warn Comiskey about the "fix" and return the money. Neither claim was substantiated. Jackson signed a confession, stating he had accepted the money, but later claimed that he didn't understand the confession, and said that the team's attorney had taken advantage of his illiteracy.

Today, many of his supporters for entry into the National Baseball Hall of Fame, look to having Pete Rose carry the torch. Once Rose is voted into the Hall, they believe, there will be a much better chance to apply pressure on Major League Baseball to also admit Jackson.

Forgiveness is a wonderful thing, and perhaps we should forgive Jackson. But forgiving a man, and putting him in the Hall of Fame, are completely different things.

As for Pete Rose, the betting odds are not in favor of him making it into the National Baseball Hall of Fame, at least in his lifetime.

Up next, Chapter 6, Pete Rose: An American Enigma.

Chapter 6

Pete Rose:
An American Enigma

"I owe baseball. Baseball don't owe me a damn thing."

— Pete Rose

"Charlie Hustle"

Pete Rose, a.k.a. *"Charlie Hustle,"* was a sports icon for almost a quarter-century. A tough and tireless ballplayer, he holds several of Major League Baseball's all-time records, including one for playing in over 500 games at five different positions.

Having rubbed elbows with twenty-five Hall of Fame players, and dozens of other immortal stars, I am convinced that Pete Rose was far less talented than several other major league players I knew.

A young Pete Rose.
(Neil Leife photo for Sports Illustrated)

Yet, his tenaciousness, hard-charging, hard playing, headfirst base running style, and competitiveness, turned Rose, the mediocre

In 1921, advertising executive Fred R. Barnard said, "One picture is worth a thousand words."

player—into the superstar "Charlie Hustle." *What a record!*

Igniter and inspirer:

In 1963, Rose hit .273, scored 101 runs, and was named Rookie of the Year. He hit .312 in 1965, and then batted over .300 in fifteen of the next seventeen seasons, leading the National League in hitting three times. As talented as the 1970s' Reds teams were, Rose was the spark plug each year.

He led the team to back-to-back World Series victories in 1975 and 1976. Rose signed with the Philadelphia Phillies as a free agent in 1979, then in 1980 he led the Phillies to their first World Series championship in their ninety-seven-year history. On August 10, 1981, he broke Stan Musial's career record for hits when he collected his 3,631st hit.

In 1984, Rose returned to the Reds after a stint with the Montreal Expos. On September 8, 1985, he tied Cobb's fifty-seven-year-old record for career hits (4,191) with two hits against the Chicago Cubs.

Pete Rose left his playing career with more hits (4,256), more times at bat (14,053), and he played in more games (3,562), than anyone in baseball history. He also had a great eye at the plate, finishing his career with more walks than strikeouts. Rose hit for a .303 average over his career and finished with three batting titles.

This is the ballplayer, now banned for life from Major League Baseball and the Hall of Fame, that so many continue to idolize and respect. Pete Rose's most prestigious record setting event took place in a game against the San Diego Padres on September 11, 1985, at Cincinnati's Riverfront Stadium. There was

a sellout crowd of 47,237 fans on hand, and millions of others watching on television.

In the bottom of the first inning, with the Padres' pitcher Eric Show on the mound, Rose stepped into the batter's box, and worked the count to two balls and one strike. Show's next pitch was a hanging slider; Rose connected and lined the ball into left center field for a single. *He did it!* He had broken Ty Cobb's all-time record as he collected hit number 4,192 of his career.

Celebration

As Rose reached first base, thousands of cameras flashed, teammates mobbed him, fireworks exploded. Marge Schott, the Reds' owner, came onto the field, gave Pete a hug and, at the wave of her hand, a beautiful, red Corvette pulled into the playing field, and slowly drove towards first base… a gift for Pete. Garry Templeton, who had taken the throw from the Padres left fielder, Carmelo Martinez, trotted over to first base, and presented the historic ball to Rose. Show, the Padres' pitcher, walked over and shook his hand. The Reds players hoisted him onto their shoulders giving out jubilant cheers.

With many fans in tears, the crowd overwhelmed their hero with a seven-minute standing ovation. He repeatedly saluted and acknowledged the crowd several times. Nobody was ready for the game to restart. The Padres' pitcher, sat down on the mound to wait. Once the celebrating ended, the game got underway. Cincinnati won with a 2–0 shutout. Rose got two hits—one a triple—in three times at-bat.

During the after-the-game celebration, President Reagan phoned and spoke with Rose on the field. Cincinnati radio broadcaster, Marty Brennaman, read over the loudspeaker, a message from Peter Ueberroth, the Commissioner of Baseball: "Not only has he [Rose] reserved a prominent spot in Cooperstown, he has reserved a special place in the heart of every fan alive today." Fans held up signs that read simply: PETE.

Whether Rose was speaking with the President of the United States; the Commissioner of Baseball; a fan in the stands; Marge Schott, the Reds' owner; one of his gambler buddies; a player on his team or on the other team, it made no difference; everyone got the same Pete Rose.

Record-breaking mistake

The Hit King, Pete Rose, was on top of the world. *But wait…* that September 11th "record-breaking" date is wrong! Record keepers in the American League had erroneously double counted a two-hit game by Cobb in 1910. Ty Cobb actually ended his career with 4,189 hits, not the well-known number of 4,191. However, Major

League Baseball still recognizes the 4,191 number, even though that count is acknowledged to be inaccurate.[i]

It's possible to love baseball without its statistics, but the game cannot be understood without them. Pete Palmer, a computer programmer, and one of the most influential baseball thinkers of the last half-century, has spent years analyzing Major League Baseball's records.

During his research, Palmer discovered a mistake in calculations of Ty Cobb's base hits records. To validate the accuracy of his finding, he reviewed the microfilm records of the American League's official scorer sheets. Palmer's research proved that Ty Cobb was given credit for two extra hits.

This mistake meant that Pete Rose actually *passed* Ty Cobb's record on September 8, 1985, in a game at Wrigley Field. The Reds' player-manager batted second that Sunday, and went two-for-five, with a pair of singles. Even though inaccurate, the official record shows he *tied* Ty Cobb's record on September 8 when he hit a fifth inning single off of Reggie Patterson. He next grounded out, and struck out, in his final two trips to the plate. The game ended in a tie when it was suspended because of darkness. (Wrigley Field was the only major league park at that time where night games were not played. Lights would not be installed until August 8, 1988.)

Did the door slam shut on Pete Rose?

During much of his twenty-six year Major League Baseball career, Pete Rose was an incessant gambler. He bet on horses, football, basketball, and practically any other game of chance that offered the thrill of winning. We also learned that Pete Rose claimed he bet on baseball without knowing how drastic the penalties would be. "You don't think you're going to get caught." *Say Pete, didn't you ever read that "Rule 21(d) that you would have passed every time you walked into any MLB clubhouse?*

111

No matter what excuses Pete Rose offered, he had committed baseball's cardinal sin; he was in violation of Major League Baseball's Rule 21(d), betting on baseball.

Serious allegations

In early 1989, as Rose was preparing his team in Florida for its April 3 opener in Cincinnati against the Los Angeles Dodgers, he discovered that his personal and business affairs were under the microscope by the federal authorities, the media, and baseball's commissioner, Peter Ueberroth.

The first inkling of Rose's difficulties came when Commissioner Ueberroth called him to New York City on February 20, 1989. Rose was accompanied to his meeting, with both Commissioner Ueberroth and Commissioner-elect Giamatti, by his attorneys Katz and Pit-cairn. Asked why he needed two lawyers, Rose responded, "There were two commissioners."

On February 23, 1989, four days after Rose's meeting with the commissioners, John M. Dowd—a trial attorney with the Washington, D.C., firm of Heron, Burchette, Ruckert & Rothwell— was retained by the Office of the Commissioner of Baseball. His group's assignment was to investigate the link between Peter Edward (Pete) Rose, manager of the Cincinnati Reds Baseball Club, and gambling; specifically, betting on Cincinnati Reds baseball.

One month (March 20) after Rose's meeting with the commissioners, Peter Ueberroth publicly acknowledged that his office was conducting a "full inquiry into serious allegations" about Pete Rose. Ueberroth said, in a carefully worded joint statement with Giamatti, "The Office of the Commissioner, which was founded to preserve the integrity of the game, has for several months been conducting a full inquiry into serious allegations involving Mr. Pete Rose. When the Oommissioner's Office has completed its inquiry, the Commissioner will consider the information presented and take whatever action is warranted by the facts consistent with the rules and procedures of major league baseball."

Media pursuit

Peter Ueberroth's dramatic announcement seeded the media clouds. The downpour that followed drenched Rose—and baseball—with a torrent of questions and stories about Rose's associations with convicted felons, his alleged huge betting losses, and handling of his lucrative memorabilia sales and autograph signings.

When asked if he had prior knowledge of Ueberroth's statement Rose replied, "Yeah."

As more questions were fired from several directions, Rose said, "That's it. No comment." He followed up by saying, "If something happens, when it happens, I'll talk about it then."

The feeding frenzy was underway; Pete Rose was under investigation. As the media kept up their relentless pursuit, the *Dayton Daily News* reported that federal investigators were looking into "tax and gambling issues" involving Rose, including income he derived from the sale of personal memorabilia.

The paper reported that Rose sold the bat and ball used when he got his record-breaking 4,192nd major league hit in 1985, to Steve Wolter, a Cincinnati collector and Rose's insurance agent, for about $175,000. Rose later told reporters that Wolter indeed had the bat. Another prominent memorabilia collector told the *Dayton Daily News* that he thought a second man, Oregon collector Dennis Walker, had—what Walker believed to be—the bat used for hit 4,192.

Walker died under mysterious circumstances in July, 1987—his body was found in a room at a Las Vegas motel, where he was staying under an assumed name. Walker had purchased various memorabilia from Rose, including the Hickok Belt (valued at

$30,000), that signified Rose's selection by 300 sportswriters and broadcasters, as the outstanding professional athlete of 1975.

The media bombs just kept being hurled: The *New York Post*, quoting an unidentified source, said, "Cincinnati police estimated that Rose owed bookies between $500,000 and $750,000."

The *Cincinnati Post* quoted a former Reds' official as saying that, "Rose had gambling debts of 'close to half a million' when Rose left the Reds in 1978, and as a free agent, he signed with the Philadelphia Phillies."

Sports Illustrated was involved in tracking down a multitude of sources, stories and "leaks" related to the investigation. A source close to the Florida Racing Commission said, "[Rose] was good for $10,000 a day. That was the amount he was betting at [Tampa Bay Downs] during spring training."

The *Boston Globe:* "Rose is a high roller at casino gaming tables. Rose once won a bundle playing baccarat in Las Vegas. The next day he bought a Porsche."

The *New York Daily News* reported that Ueberroth had disclosed his investigation only after being made aware of an upcoming March 27 *Sports Illustrated* story. *SI* reported that Ueberroth had received information that Rose may have bet on baseball games. That behavior, if substantiated, could result in Rose's suspension, and jeopardize his election to the Hall of Fame when he became eligible in 1992.

Smelling a story

The Pete Rose saga was eating up the newswires. Reporters smelled a good story. They followed the investigators into restaurants, hotel lobbies, the Cincinnati airport... everywhere. Sometimes their microphones were stuck in Dowd's face. There were TV trucks, equipped with every piece of communications technology, sitting nearby; idling in the streets.

The reporters didn't ignore Rose either. They bombarded him with questions at every opportunity. At the Reds' spring training park in Plant City, Florida, Manager Rose seemed his usual unflappable self.

He casually watched as a horde of reporters and TV crews gathered; then joked about the atmosphere they were creating. At one point Rose said, "I feel like a piece of fresh meat." All types of remarks—a few improper—were hitting the airwaves and print, and some were out-of-bounds.

Rose's rebuttal

Pete Rose chose to challenge a few of those innuendos. He said he preferred to maintain a low profile at the track to avoid attention. "I'll tell you this," he said. "No one at the track has ever seen me go to the window. The IRS casts a wary eye on bettors who send others to collect their winnings. In many cases, bettors do so to hide the income they are receiving." Rose continued, "If I do anything in this world, I overpay my income tax."

The investigation

When John Dowd sat down for a briefing in the commissioner's office he would learn that Kevin Hallinan, Major League Baseball's head of security, had already started an investigation into Pete Rose, and his connection to betting on baseball. Hallinan had a preliminary list naming a few questionable characters with whom Rose was known to be associating.

John Dowd

Gold's Gym, a place Rose frequented, and a location also suspected for steroids and cocaine dealing, was also listed as worthy of scrutiny. Other red flags developed by Hallinan and his

115

staff included an FBI "tip" about Rose's gambling habits.

Two other creditable sources also provided information that Pete Rose was betting on baseball; likely in violation of Rule 21(d). For Rose, this accusation was his worst nightmare. If proven, betting on his team was baseball's unforgivable cardinal sin; his greatest dream would be destroyed.

Rule 21 (d)

Rule 21(d) is brutal and unforgiving. Commissioner Kenesaw Mountain Landis drafted this rule in 1927, in response not only to the 1919 World Series scandal, but also to do away with the ongoing connections between gamblers and baseball players.

This rule declares "permanently ineligible" any player, umpire or baseball employee who "shall bet any sum whatsoever upon any baseball game in connection with which the bettor has a duty to perform." (The rule does not discriminate. Rose's claim that he only bet on the Reds to win is invalid.)

Within less than two weeks on the job, Dowd had identified twelve people who were willing to swear under oath that Rose had bet on baseball. As the investigation moved along, several of those individuals produced solid evidence to support their allegations: canceled checks and betting slips with handwriting believed to be Rose's.

Expert analyses would later reveal that both Rose's handwriting and his fingerprints were present on various betting slips. Dowd was able to acquire court authorization to use hidden microphone recordings. Here again, evidence against Rose was significant.

Questionable connections

As the evidence mounted against Rose, John Dowd said, "In terms of getting information, this was as easy as could be; like shooting fish in a barrel. There was a connection there that you could not miss. Lead after lead was coming in."

During the investigation, an individual known as Ron Peters moved to the forefront. Peters, a Franklin, Ohio, restaurateur, was alleged to be Rose's primary bookmaker. It was revealed that Peters' attorney had approached *Sports Illustrated* in hopes of selling Peters' story about Rose betting on baseball; the magazine declined the offer.

SI also came out with another article alleging that that it had discussed purchasing a story about Rose with Paul Janszen, a bodybuilder friend of Rose. Janszen was serving a six-month sentence in a Cincinnati halfway house for evading taxes on income derived from the sale of steroids. Again, the magazine rejected the offer.

However, another weightlifter told *SI* reporters that he had overheard Janszen placing baseball bets for Rose using a phone at Gold's Gym in the Cincinnati suburb of Forest Park. Rose was well-known at Gold's Gym, and even promoted it. Rose acknowledged that he met Janszen there, but denied ever betting on baseball.

Rose admitted that he was an avid bettor at the racetrack; where gambling is legal. He also insisted he never placed illicit bets with bookies on any sport, and also denied evading income taxes or suffering large gambling losses. Rose stood by his earlier statement, "If I do anything in this world, I overpay my income tax."

It became as if a double investigation was underway. *You know the type, two or more U.S. Congressional Committees holding hearings, and seeking out evidence on the same topic.*

Sports Illustrated had a team of top-notch investigative reporters focusing on their very own Rose case. As a show of their good faith and integrity, *SI* had already passed along to Dowd, the information they had developed regarding Ron Peters and Paul Janszen.

Yet another allegation was received by *Sports Illustrated*. This time it involved hand signals. That's right... hand signals. Rose and Janszen were allegedly exchanging hand signals during Reds games at Riverfront Stadium in Cincinnati. Two other sources close to the investigation said the signals between Janszen and Rose didn't involve placing new wagers on games, but were related to updates on the scores of other games in progress, at a time early in the 1987 season when the stadium scoreboard was not working. When asked by the Dowd investigators, Rose denied exchanging signals and said, "You can check—the scoreboard has never not worked."

However, Jon Braude, the Reds' director of information, said that for eighteen games in 1987, from April 17 through May 28, Riverfront's main scoreboard, which displayed scores of out-of-town games, was out of order. Braude said two auxiliary scoreboards intermittently provided scores.

A former employee at Gold's Gym also linked Janszen and Peters. The employee said that Tommy Gioiosa, another bodybuilder pal of Rose who once managed Gold's, and Janszen, who met Rose through Gioiosa in 1986, both placed bets on Rose's behalf. The two men, the source said, "did their betting through Ron Peters. And they did call Rose, and they did get bets from him. I know that. They would say. 'Pete, what do you want to bet?'" The source said he didn't know whether such bets were on baseball, although he said, "There was a lot of betting on baseball [in the gym]."

Obsessed?

Contrary to Rose's denials, the evidence indicated he had bet heavily through bookies. Chuck Beyersdoerfer, a close friend who also worked as a handyman for Rose from September 1985 to January 1987, said he watched Rose sit in front of three TV sets in his living room and watch three football or basketball games at once.

"He would talk about betting on the games, how much money he had on them." Beyersdoerfer said he "marveled at how Rose stayed on top of his multiple games and bets. He'd be sitting there with the TV sets, keeping track in spiral notebooks of who was winning and who was losing. Pete would bet on anything, with anybody who was in the room. He would bet on the coin toss. He would bet on who would score the most points in the first half." Other sources, who didn't want their names used, said Rose had bet on pro and college football and basketball.

Rose's passion for betting was also known throughout his team's clubhouse. "Gambling just seemed like the normal thing for Pete to do," said former Reds pitcher, Ted Power. "People expected him to say, 'I was at the track yesterday, or, Yeah, I picked the trifecta.'"

Rose solicited and received betting tips from at least one of his players, reliever Rob Murphy, who ran a computerized horse breeding business on the side, and also owned thoroughbreds. "I made him a lot of money last year," said Murphy.

Piling on!

As the discovery of new evidence and negative media reports appeared never-ending, Rose continued to voice his innocence. He couldn't understand why the media reporters had plagued him so hard from the moment the commissioner released that information about the investigation. How could they believe the rhetoric coming from others, and doubt him? Pete said, "My family felt it too. Reporters, baseball investigators, and FBI agents, were everywhere and didn't give a damn about how disruptive their actions were."

What started as "one hell of a storm" had now turned into a torrential downpour.

Standing steadfast

With volumes upon volumes of accumulated evidence, Dowd was

ready to get Rose on the record; under oath. But, where would the interview take place? The press was everywhere, and he didn't want this to turn into a media circus. After talking with authorities and scouring the area, it was decided that the deposition would take place "in secret" in the basement cafeteria of a little Catholic school in Dayton, Ohio.

Two days in a basement:

On Friday, April 21, and Saturday, April 22, 1989, Pete Rose and his attorneys met with John Dowd in the basement cafeteria of that Catholic school. Dowd's entire point of the meeting was to present a treasure trove of evidence, such that any attorney would have difficulty in proclaiming Rose's innocence.

Dowd was later quoted as saying, "I was in the hopes that Rose would see the light and we could work something out." It was not to be. Rose stood steadfast; he was innocent of all accusations. For example, when confronted with the betting sheets and told that an expert analyst had determined the handwriting on the sheets were his, Rose responded, "I couldn't tell you if that's my handwriting. I don't recognize it as my handwriting. All I can tell you is what I know. I can't disagree or agree with that. I mean I never seen that before."

With the deposition phase over, Dowd talked a little about the lighter side of his meeting. "The nuns would bring us food, including those deadly Honey Dew donuts. I remember one of Pete's lawyers falling asleep, and the other eating a lot of donuts, so basically it was just Pete and I going over all of this."

Below are word-for-word excerpts of Pete Rose's deposition on April 20-21 under questioning by baseball investigator John Dowd:

On betting on baseball:

Dowd: "On baseball, Pete, did anybody in association with you bet on baseball or talk about betting on baseball in 1984 to 1988?"

Rose: "I don't know what you mean talk about betting on baseball. No one bet baseball around me."

Dowd: "That's what I want to know. Did anybody discuss... "

Rose: "I don't understand what you mean talking about it."

Dowd: "Discuss it. Did they say, 'Hey Pete', you know, 'should I bet on the Reds today?'"

Rose: "No..."

Dowd: "Should I bet on the Dodgers? Should I bet on the Yanks? What do they look like? Who's pitching?"

Rose: "No."

Dowd: "Any... ever any discussion like that?"

Rose: "No. No way."

Dowd: "Anybody ever ask you for advice or direction as to how they ought to place bets on professional major league baseball?"

Rose: "No."

Dowd: "And I take it you didn't offer it? You never volunteered it to anybody?"

Rose: "I wouldn't know how to do it."

Dowd: "But, you didn't do it?"

Rose: "Did not do it. I did not do it."

Dowd: "Right, 1984 to 1988, you never did it?"

Rose: "No, I never did it ever. 1974. 1964. Never."

Dowd: "Fine."

Rose: "Not just '84 to '88... That's why I was sort of surprised to read the statements by Mike Fry in the *Sports Illustrated*. Or where in the hell he got those statements at."

Dowd: "And what statements were those, Pete?"

Rose: "That I... he quoted me as saying, well I like to bet on the Reds and I like to bet on baseball. This would be a good day to bet. That's a bunch of (expletive)."

On Janszen and drugs:

Dowd: "I take it you never had a conversation with him (Paul Janszen) about drugs?"

Rose: "No. No. So I think that's why he probably started hanging with me so close... It kind of seems to me that those fellows were all trying to link gambling to me because they were all in trouble with drugs... Blackmail. He said he was going to tell the commissioner I bet on baseball. He was going to kill my wife. He was going to cripple my kids... And I knew for a fact when I went to spring training this year that he was going to go to the commissioner's office."

Facts ignored

Throughout the deposition, Dowd was never confrontational, and he and Rose never seemed to exchange cross words. But both knew what was on the table; admission to the Hall of Fame. Dowd had opened the door for a possible deal. Surely Rose and his attorneys could not ignore the facts. There were volumes of physical evidence, sworn statements from gamblers, acquaintances, and others, as well as court authorized hidden microphone recordings of conversations implicating Rose in betting large sums of money on Major League Baseball games, and on games involving the Cincinnati Reds.

Coming clean?

For years, Pete Rose defiantly professed his innocence, claiming that he had never bet on baseball. As the years passed, Rose's stories of denial shifted from one tale to another. He finally admitted to betting on baseball during a January 8, 2004, interview with ABC's Charlie Gibson; after nearly two and one-half decades of steadfastly denying that it had never happened. "That was my mistake, not coming clean a lot earlier," Rose said.

Getting it wrong — again!

After all of those years of denial, and then coming clean with an admission that he had lied causes me to question Rose's motives. *Could this sudden disclosure have anything to do with the publication of his new book, My Prison Without Bars?* Rose also appeared on Dan Patrick's ESPN radio show on March 14, 2007, and made an admission related to the time when he managed the Cincinnati Reds in the 1980's, "I bet on my team every night."

He added, "I didn't bet on my team four nights a week. I bet on my team to win every night because I love my team, I believe in my team. I did everything in my power every night to win that game." To some fans, Pete was very convincing. But this isn't about his naïve defenders. It's about Rose getting it wrong... again.

Contrary to what was said during the radio interview, Rose did not bet on Reds games daily. The record that John M. Dowd's investigators created demonstrated that there were games on which he did not bet. The Dowd report included a diary of bets that Rose made on Reds games, and many others. It listed bets on 390 games overall, fifty-two of them involving the Reds, in a three-month period in 1987. Rose developed a pattern of not betting on certain games. This finding was used in rebuttal to Rose's supporters, who said it was no big deal if Rose bet on games, as long as he didn't bet on the Reds to lose.

To the Dowd team, the failure of Rose to place his bet on his team to win, meant he was likely sending a message that, on that specific day, he lacked confidence in his team winning. They believed it was a signal to his bookies that, as manager of the team, didn't think much of his team's chances that day when [a specific pitcher] was to start.

Dowd's research showed that in sixty-nine instances, Rose bet $2,500 or more on a game. Astoundingly, he lost sixty-four of those sixty-nine, which computes to a .072 success rate.[ii]

After written communications to Commissioner Manfred, via his attorneys, on February 26, 2015, and again through counsel, on April 1, 2015, the Commissioner was assured that Mr. Rose had accepted responsibility for his mistakes and their consequences, and was sorry for betting on tbaseball games. The attorneys further asserted that, as directed by Commissioner Giamatti, Mr. Rose had "reconfigured" his life.

Also, on April 1, 2015, nearly three decades after Pete Rose had signed an agreement that resulted in him being placed on the permanently ineligible list for violating Major League Rule 21(d), he reinstituted his plea for "forgiveness."

After a review of the case, Commissioner Manfred announced on Monday, December 14, 2015, that he had rejected Rose's plea for reinstatement. The Commissioner cited Rose's continued gambling, and evidence that he bet on games when he was playing for the Cincinnati Reds. Manfred made public that Pete Rose hadn't been completely honest about his gambling.

The case against Pete Rose

Once Pete Rose's gambling problems became public, he was criticized in the press, and by both his fans and fellow players. Betting on baseball was only one of his problems. He would plead guilty on April 21, 1990, to filing false income tax returns. On June 20, 1990, Pete Rose was sentenced to serve five months in a federal correctional institution.

The sentencing jurist, Judge Spiegel, explained to the filled-to-capacity courtroom, the reasoning behind his decision. "We must recognize that there are two people here: Pete Rose, the living legend, the all-time hit leader, and the idol of millions; and, Pete Rose, the individual, who appears today convicted of two counts of cheating on his taxes," the judge said. "Today, we are not dealing with the legend.

History and the tincture of time will decide his place among the all-time greats of baseball. With regard to Pete Rose, the individual, he has broken the law, admitted his guilt, and stands ready to pay the penalty."

Critical findings and rulings

On May 9, 1989, special counsel Dowd provided a 225-page report, accompanied by seven volumes of exhibits, to the commissioner. Two days later, the commissioner forwarded a copy of the above documents to Pete Rose and his counsel.

A hearing was scheduled for June 26, 1989. Peter Edward "Pete" Rose indicated he would not avail himself of the opportunity to participate in a hearing concerning the allegations against him, or otherwise offer any defense to those allegations.

On Sunday, the day prior to the scheduled hearing, in a courtroom less than two miles from Riverfront Stadium where Rose's Reds play, Hamilton County Common Pleas Court Judge, Norbert Nadel, issued a startling challenge to the authority of Baseball Commissioner Bart Giamatti.

Judge Nadel granted Rose a temporary restraining order, blocking Baseball from holding a hearing on the allegations that had been scheduled for the next day in Giamatti's New York City office.

On Monday afternoon, June 26, 1989, Judge Nadel unleashed

another blockbuster. Under orders from the Ohio Supreme Court, he released John Dowd's investigative report on Pete Rose.

The Summary of the Dowd Report indicated that Pete Rose had denied, under oath, ever betting on Major League Baseball, or associating with anyone who bet on Major League Baseball. However, the report also pointed out that the investigation had developed evidence to the contrary. Documentary evidence gathered during the course of the investigation demonstrated that Rose did bet on baseball, during the 1985, 1986, and 1987 seasons.

The evidence showed, that with few exceptions, Rose did not deal directly with bookmakers, but rather placed his bets through others. The report further cited, "No evidence was discovered that Rose bet against the Cincinnati Reds." However, evidence revealed that Pete Rose did bet on the Cincinnati Reds during the first half of the 1987 season.

Dowd's team was prepared to present a devastating amount of evidence, such as Rose's handwriting and fingerprints on betting slips, phone records, canceled checks, and a dozen individuals willing to testify that Pete Rose did in fact, bet on baseball.

According to interviews with *Sports Illustrated,* and testimony transcripts, Ron Peters, a former bookmaker, gave a compelling account of Rose's alleged involvement in baseball betting between 1985 and 1987.

Decision time

Rose acknowledged he would accept the penalty imposed on him by the commissioner and agreed not to challenge that penalty in court or otherwise. The commissioner formally imposed, "Peter Edward Rose is hereby declared permanently ineligible in accordance with Major League Rule 21(d) and placed on the Ineligible List." The Agreement allowed Rose, under Major League Rule 15(c), to apply for reinstatement. This Agreement and Resolution document was signed on August 23, 1989.

The next day, August 24, Baseball Commissioner Giamatti issued a statement: "The banishment for life of Pete Rose from baseball is the sad end of a sorry episode. One of the game's greatest players has engaged in a variety of acts which have stained the game, and he must now live with the consequences of those acts. By choosing not to come to a hearing before me, and by choosing not to proffer any testimony or evidence contrary to the evidence and information contained in the report of the Special Counsel to the Commissioner, Mr. Rose has accepted baseball's ultimate sanction, lifetime ineligibility."

On August 24, 1989, less than four years after that magnificent celebratory night on September 11, 1985, Pete Rose was banned from baseball for life, for betting on Cincinnati Reds games.

Devastating decision

On January 7, 1991, Pete Rose—Number 14 for the Cincinnati Reds and Number 01832061 at Marion Federal Prison—walked out of the minimum security lockup in Marion, Illinois, after serving five months for federal income tax evasion. With this first phase of his sentence completed, later in the day, Rose would report to Talbert House, where he would be confined in the evenings, and during days he would begin his 1,000 hours of community service at Cincinnati's inner city schools. He was also required to pay a $50,000 fine.

As Rose moved between the two facilities, he had no idea that in just three days—January 10—a special committee of ten men would get together in a midtown hotel room in New York City, and play a crucial role in sealing his fate in his quest to have his name appear on the upcoming voting ballot for election to the Hall of Fame.

The special committee, by a vote of seven to three, recommended an important change in the existing rules for election to the National Baseball Hall of Fame. This recommendation was forwarded to the Hall of Fame Board of Directors for consideration.

The announcement from the Board would be devastating to Rose. After extensive discussion, a vote was taken in which the Board ratified the resolution, passed on February 4, 1991, known today as Rule 3(E) by the Baseball Writers' Association of America (BBWAA) election rules. One major function of BBWAA is to elect players to the National Baseball Hall of Fame. As such, anyone deemed permanently ineligible by Major League Baseball, including Pete Rose, may not be considered for the honor.

The Board of Directors of the Hall of Fame, with twelve of its sixteen members present, voted unanimously to bar Rose from the ballot. It was decided that as long as he is ineligible to work in baseball, he will be ineligible for the Hall of Fame. At this point, it became obvious that the Board was so determined to block Rose—a convicted felon and gambler—that the entire group was willing to rewrite the election rule's requirements. It was interesting to note that no such rule previously existed.

NFL gambling

The National Football League (NFL) was also confronted with issues pertaining to betting on league games. On April 17, 1963, Green Bay Packers halfback, Paul Hornung—one of pro football's most glamorous stars—and Detroit Lions defensive tackle, Alex Karras —one of the game's best defensive tackles—were both suspended indefinitely by NFL Commissioner, Pete Rozell, for betting on league games, and associating with gamblers or "known hoodlums."

Unlike Rose refused to do for years, Hornung expressed immediate contrition. Swarmed by reporters on the golf course that afternoon, he said tearfully, "I made a terrible mistake. I realize that now. I am truly sorry. What else is there to say?"

Karras responded differently, insisting he had done nothing wrong.[iii]

The allegations

Hornung and Karras were accused of betting, typically in the $50 to $200 range, on NFL games. Rozelle said that Karras had placed at least six bets since 1958 of $50 each, until upping the amount to $100 on the Lions to beat the Packers in the 1962 Thanksgiving Day game, and on the Packers to beat the Giants in the NFL Championship game.

As for Hornung, the commissioner indicated that he had placed several bets through a friend on the West Coast over the course of his career.

Five other Detroit players were fined $2,000 each. Commissioner Rozelle had concluded that they were each guilty of a single violation of the league's gambling policy.

While the suspensions of Hornung and Karras were indefinite, Rozelle indicated that they could be reviewed, although no earlier than the conclusion of the 1963 season. The reactions of the two players carried over into their behavior over the course of the ensuing year.

Hornung remained contrite and kept in contact with the league office, clearing his activities (such as attending the Kentucky Derby), and seeking a path toward reinstatement.

Karras remained defiant, and refused to sell the interest he had in a bar, that had first drawn the attention of the Detroit police to the defensive tackle's association with known gamblers. The Lions were fined for not adequately following up on the reports they had received from the police, and for allowing unauthorized individuals who were suspected gamblers, including one of Karras' partners in the business, to sit on the team's bench during games.

In early January, 1964, Karras, concerned about his chances of being reinstated, finally sold his interest in the bar.

Eleven months after the suspensions, on March 16, 1964, the NFL released a five paragraph statement announcing that Hornung and Karras had been reinstated.[iv]

Appeals

In 2003, fourteen years after he was made ineligible for the Hall of Fame, Commissioner Bud Selig took up Rose's application for reinstatement, igniting once again an intense debate about Rose's legacy and baseball's long-standing zero tolerance policy on gambling. Selig took no action on the application. To quote one source, "He just sat on it." *Another, "Sorry, Pete."*

Ron Manfred, in his second month as commissioner, on February 26, 2015, received Pete Rose's request for reinstatement and removal from MLB's permanently ineligible list.

Commissioner Manfred said he would consider the case for reinstatement. But, he would need to review the Dowd report, as well as Baseball's constitution, along with the actual agreement between Rose and former Commissioner Giamatti.

Ten months later, on Monday, December 14, 2015, Commissioner Manfred announced that he had *rejected Pete Rose's plea for reinstatement.* In expressing the reasoning behind his decision, Commissioner Manfred cited a number of issues, including the following:

- "It is not at all clear to me that Mr. Rose has a grasp of the scope of his violations of Rule 21. He claims not to remember significant misconduct detailed in the Dowd Report and corroborated by Michael Bertolini's betting notebook. While Mr. Rose claims that he only bet on Baseball in 1987, the

Dowd Report concluded that he also bet on Baseball in 1985 and 1986".

- "Based on review of the Bertolini Notebook (which shows that Mr. Rose bet on Baseball during the 1986 season), I am convinced that the findings set forth in the Dowd Report are credible. Mr. Rose's public and private comments, including his initial admission in 2004, provide me with little confidence that he has a mature understanding of his wrongful conduct, that he has accepted full responsibility for it, or that he understands the damage he has caused."

- "As I understand it, Mr. Rose has never seriously sought treatment for either of the two medical conditions[v] described so prominently in his 2004 book,[vi] and in Dr. Fang's report.[vii] I am also not convinced that he has avoided the type of conduct and associations that originally led to his placement on the permanently ineligible list."

Showed no remorse

Perhaps the worst of Pete Rose's pigheadedness was the fact that, even when he had his chance to plead his case before the commissioner, he vehemently denied betting on the Cincinnati Reds. (Although in an interview—some fifteen years later—Rose half-heartily admitted to such betting.[viii])

Furthermore, the commissioner noted that Rose showed no remorse about his gambling; he acknowledged that he had continued to bet on horses and Major League Baseball.

Breaking news

For nearly three decades, Pete Rose has told only one story: He never bet on baseball while he was a player. Yet, he admitted in 2004, after almost 15 years of denials—many under oath—that he had placed bets on baseball, but he insisted it only took place when he was the manager.

The timing for Rose, who played in seventy-two games in 1986, wasn't great. In April, 2015, Rose appeared on Michael Kay's ESPN New York 98.7 FM radio program, and repeated his denial that he bet on baseball while he was a player, "Never bet as a player: That's a fact."

However, two months later (June 2015), *Outside the Lines* published an article that sent shock waves throughout Rose's league of loyal fans: Pete Rose bet extensively on baseball—and on the Cincinnati Reds—as he racked up the last hits of a record-smashing career in 1986.

Outside the Lines had uncovered a collection of documents that go beyond the evidence presented in the 1989 Dowd report. The documents provided the first written record that Rose had bet while he was still a player. Next, the magazine tracked down two of the postal inspectors who conducted the raid on Michael Bertolini's (former Rose associate) home in 1989, and asked them to review the documents. Former Supervisor, Craig Barney, and former Inspector, Mary Flynn, said the records were indeed copies of the [Bertolini] notebook they seized.

"When the case began, it didn't look particularly enticing," Barney said. "The postal inspector's office in Brooklyn, New York, had received a complaint that a man in Staten Island had failed to return goods to paying customers that was supposed to have been autographed." The man's name was Michael Bertolini, and the business he ran out of his home was called Hit King Marketing, Inc. "It was a mere 'failure to render [services]' complaint. We didn't know anything about Bertolini or his connection [to Rose]. If the accusation was true, it would constitute mail fraud, but the agents had no probable cause to search Bertolini's house", said Barney, who is now retired.

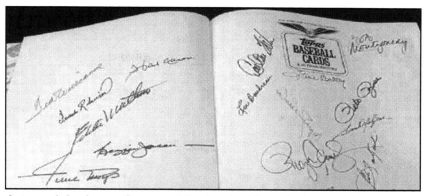

Autograph book page from a notebook seized from the home of former Rose associate, Michael Bertolini, during a raid by the U.S. Postal Inspection Service in October 1989.

Barney sent an agent to drive by the address. There was a 'For Sale' sign out front, the agent told him. So Barney and Flynn, posing as a couple looking for a home, called a real estate agent and were given a guided tour of Bertolini's house.

"It was such a mess. There was stuff everywhere," Barney said. "Bats, balls, books, and papers were scattered all over." It looked to them as if Bertolini had been signing memorabilia with the forged names of some of the most famous baseball players in history: Willie Mays, Hank Aaron, Duke Snider, Mike Schmidt and Pete Rose. It reeked of fraud," Barney said.[ix]

The two inspectors spotted an item that a complainant said had not been returned. That gave them probable cause to seek a search warrant. On October 13, a few days after the undercover house tour, and after obtaining a search warrant, they searched Bertolini's home and found evidence that would lead to numerous convictions. Barney said, "But one item stood out."

In a box of papers in the basement was a spiral notebook filled with handwritten entries. It was immediately clear that the many notations of 'PETE' in the pages represented Pete Rose. "There were numbers and dates and it was a book for sports betting." Barney said, "I was taken aback." Flynn, who said her first reaction was, "Holy mackerel," said they asked Bertolini about the notebook. "He wasn't forthcoming with much information," she said, "but he did acknowledge to me it was records of bets he made for Pete Rose."

Bertolini offered his version of the raid during his sentencing hearing in U.S. District Court in Brooklyn six years later (he served 14 months for tax fraud and a concurrent assault sentence): "I got a call at the place where I was working at the time from my brother, and he says, 'You should come home. There's a bunch of government people here, and they're here for you.' At the time, I think it was Mary Flynn of the postal inspector's office who got on the phone and said, 'We're here,' and she told me why and so forth. They took any records I had whatsoever, and they took different personal belongings and memorabilia from my home."

Bertolini Notebook

Although the 1989 raid on Bertolini's house received immediate news coverage, nothing about a betting book would be publicized for another five years. After Bertolini pleaded guilty and received a federal prison sentence, *Sports Illustrated, The New York Times,* ESPN, and other news organizations, filed freedom of information requests with the U.S. Attorney's Office, seeking access to the notebook. All were denied on the grounds that the notebook had been introduced as a grand jury exhibit, and contained information "concerning third parties who were not of investigative interest." *Outside the Lines* again applied, unsuccessfully, for access to the notebook, but learned it had been transferred to the National Archives under a civil action titled "United States v. One Executive Tools Spiral Notebook." Two small boxes of other items confiscated in the postal raid on Bertolini's house were also relocated with the notebook, including autographed baseballs and baseball cards.

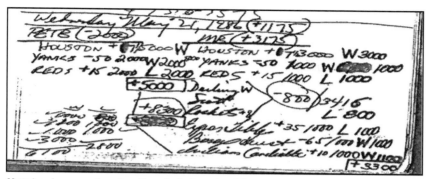

Notebook page showing Rose's bets seized from the home of former Rose associate, Michael Bertolini, during a raid by the U.S. Postal Inspection Service in October 1989.

Outside the Lines gained access to, and examined, the Bertolini memorabilia kept in the National Archives' New York office, but the betting book—held apart from everything else—was off-limits. A U.S. Attorney's Office internal memorandum from 2000 requesting the notebook's transfer, said Bertolini's closed file has "sufficient historical or other value to warrant its continued preservation by the United States Government." This memorandum listed among its attachments, a copy of the notebook. However, a copy of the memorandum provided by the National Archives had no attachments, plus a section was redacted.

All documents obtained by *Outside the Lines,* which reflect betting records from March through July, 1986, showed no evidence that Rose, who was a player-manager in 1986, bet against his team. However, they provided a vivid snapshot of how extensive Rose's betting life was in 1986:

- In the time covered in the notebook—March through July, 1986—Rose bet on at least one MLB team on 30 different days. (It was impossible to count the exact number of times he bet on baseball games because not every day's entries are legible.)

- On twenty-one of the days, it's clear [Rose] bet on baseball, he gambled on the Reds, including on games in which he played.

  Mary Flynn, the former postal inspector said, "I wish I had been able to use it [the notebook] all those years [Rose] was denying he bet on baseball. He's a liar."

To John Dowd, one of the most compelling elements of the newly uncovered evidence was that it supported the charge that Rose was betting with mob-connected bookies through Bertolini. Dowd's investigation had established that Rose was hundreds of thousands of dollars in debt at the time he was banished from the game.

"Bertolini nails down the connection to organized crime on Long Island and New York. And that is a very powerful problem," Dowd said.

Ultimate conflicts

In his final report on the Rose investigation, Special Counsel John Dowd described why gambling is baseball's cardinal sin. In one excerpt the report stated: "Betting on one's own team gives rise to the ultimate conflict of interest in which the individual player/bettor places his personal financial interest above the interests of the team."

Mea Culpa

Americans will give a second chance to almost anyone, provided that they are willing to apologize, sincerely or not. Most of the time, a publicly issued *mea culpa* will make up for almost any sin. I have written three books on Major League Baseball. During my appearances at bookstores, fan club functions, and at various book and author expos, I have listened to numerous individuals voice their opinions about Pete Rose, and his campaign to get into the Hall of Fame. Most are on Pete's side.

Yet, beyond Pete's "Charlie Hustle" image, little is known about what actually happened. Of those unfamiliar with the real facts, the majority clings to the position: "Pete never bet against the Reds, so he should not be disqualified."

Denials and more

I have read a number of stories and articles about Pete Rose. I have also listened to his nearly fifteen years of denials, read the Dowd Report to the Commissioner, and listened to his 2004 "admission" interview with Charlie Gibson on ABC-TV. During the Gibson interview, Rose finally admitted that he placed bets on baseball, but he insisted it was only when he was a manager.

In April 2015, Rose repeated his denial, this time on Michael Kay's ESPN New York 98.7 FM radio show. Rose said he bet on baseball while he was a manager. "Never bet as a player: That's a fact," he said.

Then on June 22, 2015, ABC News headlined another explosive Pete Rose story, "New documents obtained by *Outside the Lines* indicate Rose bet extensively on baseball—and on the Cincinnati Reds—as he racked up the last hits of a record-smashing career in 1986."

Bertolini's notebook provided the first written evidence that Rose bet [1986] while he was still on the field. Rose's old standby claim: "I never bet on the Reds as a player." *More evidence of Pete Rose's lies, I thought.*

To those who ask, "Why be so tough on 'Charlie Hustle'? After all, Pete Rose only bet on his team to win." Well, let's look at a few facts:

- The relevant portion of the Major League Baseball Rulebook's, Rule 21(d) is very clear: "Any player, umpire, or club or league official or employee, who shall bet any sum whatsoever upon any baseball game in connection with which the bettor has a *duty to perform* shall be declared permanently ineligible."

- The above rule is *posted in every clubhouse* throughout Major League Baseball. Simple. No exceptions, as it should be. One strike and you're out. None of the previous fourteen players who have been declared permanently ineligible by Major League Baseball have ever been reinstated.

- For nearly fifteen years, Pete Rose *denied under oath,* ever betting on Major League Baseball, or associating with anyone who bet on MLB. However, the Dowd investigation developed evidence to the contrary. Findings demonstrated that Pete Rose did bet on baseball, and in particular, on Cincinnati Reds Baseball Club games, during the 1985, 1986 and 1987 seasons. Furthermore, Dowd's report named those gamblers with whom Rose placed bets on baseball. Rose admitted placing bets on football and basketball games, but denied placing any bets on Cincinnati's baseball games when he was a player, even though there was handwriting and fingerprint evidence to the contrary.

- The Dowd Report presented *substantial evidence that Rose did bet on baseball games.* It cited that Rose was betting on approximately five to ten basketball, football, hockey, and baseball games every day—at about $2,000 a game. In one month, Rose lost more than $67,000, and he was often deeply in debt to bookies—at one point, he allegedly owed a Staten Island bookie $200,000. Part of the report's enormous exhibit section, used to support claims that Rose did illegally bet on baseball, included such contents as telephone and bank records, betting records, and transcripts of interviews with Rose, and other witnesses.

- On August 24, 1989, Commissioner Bart Giamatti announced that Pete Rose—the game's all-time hits leader—was banned from baseball for life for gambling on the sport. In response to

Giamatti's ban, *Rose insisted at the time, "I don't think I have a gambling problem at all."*

- Despite Rose's continued denials relating to the charges against him, he voluntarily accepted a permanent place on baseball's ineligible list. Allegedly, *Rose agreed to his ban in large part so the investigation would stop*. As Matt Snyder from CBS *SportsLine* put it: "We'll never know what more the investigation would have found and revealed, but we do know Rose wanted badly enough for it to stop that he cut the deal and volunteered to be banned from baseball for life."

- According to baseball's rules, Rose could have applied for reinstatement after one year, but waited until 1992, three years later, to first apply. He again applied in 1997. Critics point out that *if Rose had nothing to hide, he would have had no reason to remain silent,* and accept an agreement to voluntarily withdraw from the sport. Commissioners Vincent and Selig never responded to Rose's reinstatement efforts.

My thoughts

While I never met Pete Rose, I always admired his apparent dedication to the game and style of play. And, yes, I was disheartened when I first learned that hisHall of Fame eligibility was in jeopardy. His gambling issues, which he steadfastly denied for many years—several times under oath—were of serious concern.

Initially, I wanted to see this great player's plaque hanging in Cooperstown, but today I believe such an honor would be a travesty. Yes, he is a baseball hero to so many people. While writing this chapter, I decided to "test the waters" by asking a number of friends what they thought about Pete Rose being banned.

Not surprisingly, the majority believed that he should be in the Hall of Fame. But they knew very little, if anything, about his gambling habits, his decades of lies accompanied by half-hearted admissions, the rock-solid evidence against him, or his imprisonment for IRS violations.

It is not my intention to attempt to sway anyone's opinion; each can draw their own conclusions. However, I do think that it is important that everyone understand the basic facts of the Pete Rose situation. Within this chapter, I have tried to accurately present the most relevant facts. And, what I found was not good. I believe that Pete Rose made his second biggest mistake, when confronted with all of that undisputable evidence the John Dowd investigators had collected, he chose to lie/ignore it. Pete's first huge mistake was betting on baseball; specifically, on the Cincinnati Reds. He knew the rules and what was at stake. It didn't matter that he *swore up and down,* claiming that he only bet on his team to win.

To quote John Dowd, "The implications for baseball are terrible. [The mob] had a mortgage on Pete while he was a player and manager."

I close this chapter by begging, "Pete, say it ain't so." He did, but he was lying.

Chapter 7

Juicing the Game: The Steroids Era

"When I taught other players how to use steroids, no one lifted a finger to stop me."
                                        – Jose Canseco

Path to superpower

It was May 22, 1998, the National League's season was less than two months old, and Mark McGwire had already hit twenty home runs. His pace was ahead of Babe Ruth when he hit 60 home runs in 1927, and ahead of Roger Maris when he hit 61 to break Ruth's record in 1961. The media, fans, and most players were anticipating that McGwire would break baseball's most celebrated record.

By game time, the majority of the sellout crowd of over 43,000 had worked their way into their seats in the Cardinals' Busch Stadium. McGwire had brought a level of excitement to the game that had been missing since the Cardinals' "Stan the Man" Musial became the oldest player to ever hit three home runs in one game. Watching McGwire was making the game fun again.

The media was enthralled with the man sporting red hair, a

freckled, weather-beaten face,
and a smile that seemed to invite
conversation. McGwire was also
huge. He had shoulders as wide as
Paul Bunyan's, and forearms that
matched those of Popeye.

Many stood and watched in awe
as the Cardinals' first baseman,
number 25, stepped up to the
plate to take his turn at batting
practice. At six-feet, five-inches,
and weighing 260 pounds, he was
solid muscle, a man of exceptional
size and power.

Along with those watching
from the stands, a lone San Francisco Giants' player, Barry
Bonds, secretly watched from the visiting team's dugout. He saw
ten batting practice pitches sail deep into the stands, smiled,
and assured himself that he had identified the source of Mark
McGwire's power.

When that Friday game was over, the scorecard would show that
Bonds went one-for-four; a double. McGwire had a much better
game. He went one-for-three; a home run in the sixth inning with a
man on base, driving in two runs. The final score was 4–3, St. Louis
Cardinals over the San Francisco Giants.

In August, when McGwire had already recorded forty-three homers,
an *Associated Press* reporter spotted a bottle of androstenedione
(Andro) in his locker, at Busch Stadium. The reporter's curiosity
would reveal that Andro was a testosterone booster, and while
legal, it had the same muscle building effects as anabolic steroids, a
drug outlawed in 1991 by the U.S. Congress.

Mark McGwire finished the 1998 season with 70 home runs,

including five in his last three games. When the final results were tabulated, McGwire closed his season four home runs ahead of Sammy Sosa's sixty-six, a record that would be broken three seasons later, in 2001. Barry Bonds hit seventy-three home runs that year. Yes, Bonds had discovered the source of McGwire's amazing power.

Juicing the Game

Andro had been banned by the International Olympic Committee, the National Collegiate Athletic Association, and the National Football League. However, Major League Baseball had no rules against the use of steroids. It also possessed a liberal attitude about cheating. Between throwing illegal pitches such as spitballs, corking bats, and using unscrupulous methods to steal the opposing team's signs, several ways of cheating can be traced back to the game's earliest days. Teams did whatever they could to get an advantage. The message was clear, cheaters will cheat. That's what they do.

Steroids and sports

Since the beginning of competitive sports, athletes have always searched for a way to gain an advantage over their competitors. Many relied on performance-enhancing drugs (PEDs) as they have been around forever—caffeine is one of the oldest known stimulants. As for baseball, there is a legend that back in 1889, Pud Galvin, a pitcher for the Pittsburg Alleghenys (later known as the Pittsburgh Pirates), used a form of testosterone derived from animals, most notably dogs and guinea pigs, as a strength enhancer.

There is also evidence that during World War II, amphetamines were given to U.S. military personnel to help them better perform their duties. Once discharged from service, a number of veterans returned with their supply of amphetamines, and discovered that these stimulants helped to elevate their performance in athletic events. But the biggest connection between athletes and drugs occurred when the team physician for the U.S. weightlifting team at the 1956 world championships in Vienna, observed the Soviet team being injected with a substance he believed to be testosterone; which was legal at that time.

The team's doctor decided to level the playing field by fighting fire with fire. The cold war between the United States and Russia was joined by the chemical warfare of performance-enhancing drugs.

Getting amped

The highest-profile case of drug usage at the Olympics occurred in 1988 in Seoul, South Korea. On September 24, 1988, Canadian sprinter, Ben Johnson, took his position in Lane 6.

When the starter's pistol fired at 1:30 p.m., Johnson was off, and by the ten-meter mark, he had more than a one foot lead over his closest competitor. Seventy thousand people stood in Olympic Stadium and cheered as Johnson's superior muscles ramped up to an incredible 5.02 strides per second at the forty-meter mark.

With fifteen meters to go, he was so far ahead that he stopped pumping his arms, and still glided to a world record 9.79-second time. With the race won, there was only one more formality. He had to give a urine sample.

Three days later, on September 27, 1988, Ben Johnson was stripped of his gold medal after testing positive for anabolic steroids. Dejected, he left for the airport, and caught a flight back to Toronto.

Nearly fifteen years after the Seoul Olympics, it was discovered that several United States track athletes had also tested positive for drugs before those games.

Steroid Nation

As far back as the early 1960s, I remember encountering living proof that steroids and other performance-enhancing drugs, were commencing to take center stage in the sports world. I was working part-time as a fitness instructor for Vic Tanny Gyms, in the Washington, D.C. area, when I first became aware of the muscle-building power of steroids and other PEDs.

At that time, professional wrestling was a popular nationwide sporting event, both on television and before live audiences in local sports arenas. Our gym, on Connecticut Avenue, was a preferred training destination for many professional wrestlers, and top-notch bodybuilders.

So, I got to know several of these muscular men fairly well. We casually talked about such trivial things as "eating healthy," and which muscle-building supplements were the best. At times, our talks would shift to a little gossip about what was happening around the circuit. During these talks I got my first verbal introduction to the Steroid Nation.

Almost without exception, the hottest news revolved around the outstanding progress of a few bodybuilders who were training at Muscle Beach in Venice, California, and at a couple of progressive gyms on the East Coast. Naturally, I was curious, and fired off a few questions as to what was taking place. The answers I heard had to do with performance-enhancing drugs, known as anabolic steroids. My sources said that this "supplement," and others, were readily available for sale by a few local "gym rats" who were pushing the drugs.

Arnold Schwarzenegger –1960s

I was told that a number of weightlifters and bodybuilders were taking them regularly to improve their physical performance and build up their bodies. Steroids were also proving to help increase muscle mass, while decreasing fat.

Talk was that almost all high-level competitive bodybuilders were taking steroids in the weeks leading up to contests. Winning at any cost, made it all worthwhile.

One day, a well proportioned and muscular man, whom I had never seen before, stopped by our gym for a workout. When introduced, I recognized his name, "Mighty Atlas," a professional wrestler. He often demonstrated feats of strength before his matches, bending iron bars, snapping chains, ripping phone books, lifting an anvil with his teeth while someone whacked it with a hammer. "Atlas" was also known for performing 500-pound bench presses. This amazing feat I wanted to see!

So, I talked him into doing the lift that had made him a legend in the world of pro wrestling. For safety, I "spotted" his lift. He did it. Impressed? You bet I was impressed! I had never observed such amazing strength. (In 2013, Tiny Meeker—five-feet, nine-inches tall, and weighing 320 pounds—bench pressed 1,102 pounds, making him the only man in the world to officially bench press over 1,100 pounds. Meeker is also acknowledged as a twenty-five-time *drug-free* bench press World Champion.)

Weeks later, another attention-getting visitor came into the gym— a champion bodybuilder. Since he was somewhat of a "fixture" on the covers of two or three national magazines, I shall refer to him only as, "Mr. Amazing." While his muscular body was amazing, his real claim to fame were his huge twenty-two-inch-plus biceps. They were bigger than a normal man's thigh.

Back then, even the top nationwide bodybuilders' biceps never exceeded nineteen inches, with the exception of the great Leroy Colbert's arms. "Mr. Amazing's" massive body muscles and protruding veins, gave him away. I wondered, if I looked closer in places I didn't want to look, would I see track marks? As "Mr. Amazing" went through his lifting routine, I tried to ignore the way his veins throbbed in his neck; a sight I shall never forget.

Those two exceptional strength exhibitions were my first introductions to a class of Herculean athletes; one free of steroids, and the other questionable. By the time we entered the 1970s, it was common knowledge that steroids, as well as amphetamines, were being used by athletes in most major U.S. sports. The use of steroids had become so widespread that their oversight was assigned to the FDA, through the passing of a 1981 amendment to the Food, Drug, and Cosmetic Act requiring that steroids be prescribed by a physician.

Baseball's drug connection

Throughout history, baseball has maintained its position at the pentacle of American sports. Sure, along the way as it moved into the twenty-first century, the game hit some tough ruts in the road: Moses Fleetwood Walker, the first African-American to play Major League Baseball was banned from playing in 1884 because of his race; four Louisville Grays' players were banned for life for throwing a game back in 1876; 1919 World Series scandal; the Pete Rose betting scandal; the reserve clause/free agency dispute; and the MLB Players Association's 1994-1995 strike.

Yet, on the horizon was the most devastating baseball scandal of all—doping. Steroid and PED usage had been whispered about as early as the 1980s, but baseball's officials had chosen to ignore the growing number of doping reports. It was now getting out of control.

Cat's out of the bag

Then along came a player of Herculean proportion, Jose Canseco of the Oakland Athletics. Canseco had burst into the major leagues during mid season in 1985. His spectacular entry changed the sport in more ways than one. No player before Canseco had possessed his combination of speed and power. He batted an impressive .302 in his rookie season. During Canseco's first full season in 1986, he hit thirty-three home runs, and won American League's Rookie of the Year award.

In 1988, Canseco became the first player in Major League Baseball history to hit forty-two home runs, and steal forty bases in the same season. He also won that year's American League's Most Valuable Player Award.

Next, were the rumors: Almost instantaneously, Canseco became the first baseball player to become the subject of media conjecture about the possible use of steroids. As speculation spread, and while Canseco and his team were playing at Fenway Park in Boston, the Red Sox's fans taunted him for his alleged use of steroids during the 1988 American League Championship Series.

It was well-known that many athletes using steroids were also prone to injuries; Canseco was no exception. His injury-plagued career forced him into retirement. He finished his illustrious sixteen-year major league career with 462 home runs, six All-Star selections, one American League MVP Award, and two World Series championships. However, Canseco's greatest effect on baseball would materialize after he hung up his cleats.

Juiced

On February 21, 2005, Jose Canseco's book, *Juiced*, hit the bookstores, and drew national attention from major media outlets. An instant best seller, *Juiced* wasn't the average book you would expect from any professional athlete, especially one authored by a big league baseball superstar. Described as a tell-all, it painted an alarming picture of Canseco's longtime steroid use. He also dared to cross over to the secret side of the game by claiming that the abuse of performance-enhancing drugs was virtually ubiquitous among baseball's top stars. Canseco wrote, "The challenge is not to find a top player who has used steroids. The challenge is to find a top player who *hasn't*."

Canseco also criticized, what he called, Major League Baseball's politics and double standards. He continued by asking such hardball questions as: "Is it cheating to do what everyone wants you to do?" "Are players the only ones to blame for steroids when Donald Fehr, [executive director], and the other bosses of the Major League Players' Association, fought to make sure players wouldn't be tested for steroids?"

Canseco didn't let up, and opened the floodgates with even more embarrassing questions: "Is it all that secret when the owners of the game put out the word that they want home runs and excitement, making sure everyone—from trainers to managers to clubhouse attendants—understands that whatever it is the players are doing to become superhuman, they sure ought to keep it up?"[ii]

Canseco also bragged about being known as "the godfather of steroids in baseball." He insisted that he "introduced steroids into the big leagues back in 1985, and taught other players how to use steroids and growth hormones."[iii]

Less than one month later, on March 18, 2005, the allegations in Canseco's book caused the U.S. Congress to start formal hearings on steroid use in baseball. Henry Waxman, a Democrat, and the ranking minority member of the committee, said baseball wasn't doing enough to curtail their use. "We're long past the point where we can count on Major League Baseball to fix its own problems."

Investigation

On March 30, 2006, one year after Canseco's tell-all book, Major

League Baseball announced that George Mitchell, the former U.S. Senate majority leader from Maine, (who also served as a director for the Boston Red Sox, and a chairman of The Walt Disney Company) would head a panel to investigate past steroid use by major league players.

The focus of the investigation would commence with the year 2002. Mitchell, at his request, was also given the authority to investigate anything, or any time, that was relevant to understanding the problem of steroids in baseball.

The Report

After twenty months of investigation, and interviews with over 700 witnesses in the United States, Canada, and the Dominican Republic, the *Mitchell Report* was released on December 13, 2007.

The 409-page report said the investigators found a serious drug culture within baseball, and a widespread problem that touched every one of the thirty major league teams. Questionable illegal drugs included steroids and human growth hormones; some of which could not be detected by standard urine tests.

Mitchell also named dozens of players—current and former—who had illegally used performance-enhancing drugs to different degrees. The report included a list of recommendations regarding the handling of past illegal drug use and future prevention strategies. (In addition, Canseco's *Juiced* was cited in the *Mitchell Report* a total of 105 times.)

Blame game

The report placed blame on nearly everyone involved in baseball over the past two decades, including officials in the commissioner's office, the players' union, individual players, and club owners. "There was a collective failure to recognize the problem as it emerged and to deal with it early on," Mitchell concluded. His report was especially tough on the players, the vast majority of whom refused to cooperate with the investigation.

Even today, the struggle to eliminate illegal steroids and other PEDs in baseball, and other sports, remains an ongoing battle. Since 1986, drug testing has been subject to collective bargaining in Major League Baseball.

For many years, the Players Association opposed mandatory random drug testing of its members for steroids or other substances, citing concerns for the privacy rights of players. From the owners' prospective, this was not a priority issue worthy of special attention.

Furthermore, Mitchell reported, the Players Association was largely uncooperative: (1) it rejected requests for relevant documents. (2) It permitted only one interview with its executive director, Donald Fehr; Mitchell's request for an interview with its chief operating officer, Gene Orza, was refused; (3) It refused Mitchell's request to interview the director of the Montreal laboratory that analyzes drug tests under baseball's drug program, but did permit her to provide a letter addressing a limited number of issues. (4) Mitchell sent a memorandum to every active player in Major League Baseball, encouraging them to contact Mitchell or his staff if he had any relevant information. The Players Association sent out a companion memorandum that effectively discouraged players from cooperating. Not one player contacted Mitchell in response to his memorandum. (5) Mitchell received allegations of the illegal possession or use of performance-enhancing substances by a number of current players. Through their representative, the Players Association, Mitchell asked each of them to meet with him so that he could provide them with information about the allegations, and give them a chance to respond. Almost without exception, they declined to meet or talk.

Serious problem

Mitchell concluded the problem was serious. "The illegal use of performance-enhancing substances poses a serious threat to the integrity of the game."

Eighty-nine MLB players were named in the report as having allegedly used steroids, HGH or other performance-enhancing drugs. He specifically cited that widespread use by players of such substances unfairly disadvantages the honest athletes who refuse to use them, and raises questions about the validity of baseball records.

In addition, because they are breaking the law, users of these substances are vulnerable to drug dealers who might seek to exploit their knowledge through threats intended to affect the outcome of games, or otherwise threaten players or officials. He also documented his concerns related to serious health and mental issues, and the harmful impact the use of these drugs could have on young athletes.

Mitchell's group also reported hearing from many former players who believed it was grossly unfair that some players were using performance enhancing substances to gain an advantage. One former player said that, "One of the biggest complaints among players was that a guy using steroids was taking the player's spot."

Beating the system

According to various sources, prior to the policy of mandatory random drug testing getting underway in Major League Baseball, players were moving away from oil-based steroids that stay in the body for a long time, to water-based steroids that clear the body faster. Because human growth hormones cannot be detected in standard urine tests, many players switched to them, even after concluding that they were less effective than steroids.

Other concerns cited within the Summary Section of the Mitchell Report included:

- Reports that some players received advance notice of testing. One example claimed that upcoming test notifications may be known between one and two weeks in advance.[iv]

- At the onset, mandatory random drug testing—the single most important step taken so far to combat the problem—was delayed for years by the opposition from the Players Association.[v]

In his report, Mitchell stated that "a principal goal of his investigation was to bring to a close this troubling chapter in baseball's history, and to use the lessons learned from the past to prevent the future use of performance enhancing substances."[vi]

Unfortunately, Mr. Mitchell's goal must be classified, at best, as a small step forward, and little more. Shortly afterwards, two significant banned-PED scandals would emerge.

The BALCO scandal

The Bay Area Laboratory Co-operative (BALCO) was a San Francisco Bay Area business which allegedly supplied banned anabolic steroids to professional athletes. The BALCO scandal began as two separate, independent investigations: one by federal agents in California looking into BALCO, and one by investigators for the U.S. Anti-Doping Agency working on a tip from an anonymous source. BALCO was believed by many to be behind the biggest drugs scandal in athletic history.

A grand jury investigation got underway on October 23, 2003. Dozens of high-profile athletes were subpoenaed to testify. The investigation exposed the systematic use of steroids and human growth hormones by elite athletes in several sports disciplines, including baseball, football, cycling, and track and field. This lab allegedly supplied Barry Bonds, Jason Giambi, Gary Sheffield, and a bunch of other top athletes with designer steroids.[vii]

The Biogenesis scandal

Biogenesis ran a close second to BALCO as the biggest doping scandal in baseball.

In 2013, Major League Baseball was hit with major scandal when the *Miami New Times* broke the story that Biogenesis, an anti-aging clinic in South Florida, had supplied human growth hormone, and other performance-enhancing drugs, to several high-profile players.

The Biogenesis scandal would have never become public if Porter Fischer, a former employee of the clinic (closed in late 2012), had not turned over boxes of documents to the *Miami New Times*. While the handwritten records did not definitively connect baseball players to drug use—athletes were often referred to by nicknames— MLB took the allegations seriously and purchased the records. The league then sued Biogenesis founder Tony Bosch, and eventually reached a deal with him to cooperate with its investigation.

According to whistleblower Fischer, the number of athletes linked to Biogenesis extended far beyond what had been reported. "In just the four years that I know, it's got to be well over a hundred, easy," he told ESPN's *Outside the Lines*. "It's almost scary to think about how many people have gone through [Bosch's clinic], and how long he's gotten away with this." Fischer told ESPN that athletes from the NBA, boxing, tennis, and mixed martial arts had also received drugs from Biogenesis.

It was troubling to note that none of the thirteen players sanctioned was identified by the drug testing program that MLB claims as the most effective in sports. It was also no surprise to find that the lack of cooperation between the Players Association and MLB, after the Biogenesis case, was as lacking as reported in the *Mitchell Report.*

Playing naked

Today, steroids and other PEDs have a long, and documented, history in baseball. It's no secret that players, and their reliance on drugs, has grown to alarming proportions. So popular is the use of these drugs, that some players have a catchphrase for those not taking some form of PEDs, or other stimulants: *playing naked.*

Of course, there are varying degrees of nakedness, but the fact remains that popping pills such as Ritalin, shooting steroids or other type of stimulants, or gulping amphetamine capsules, better known as greenies—is as routine to many ballplayers as taking batting practice.

According to Ken Caminiti, a National League MVP player, who admitted to having taken amphetamines as well as steroids during his fifteen year career, there were some teams on which almost everyone used some type of stimulant: "You hear it all the time from teammates, 'You're not going to play naked are you?' Even the guys who are against greenies may be popping twenty-five caffeine pills, and they're up there [at bat] with their hands shaking. This game is so whacked out that guys will take anything to get an edge. You got a pill that will make me feel better? Let me have it."

MLB actions or inaction?

I was in the dugout when such great homerun hitters as Mickey Mantle, Ted Williams, and a younger Harmon Killebrew took their turns at the plate. Therefore, I refuse to accept the rhetoric of those Major League Baseball officials, when they spew claims about thinking things were normal when *average size* players started appearing in the daily lineups, a year or so later, with behemoth gains in muscle size. Or when several obviously *bulked-up* players such as Mark McGwire, Sammy Sosa, and Barry Bonds are blasting baseballs far out of the park at an unparalleled rate. Equally amazing was seeing a number of previously average players—with average talents and power—suddenly surpassing their personal bests in home runs and/or pitching speed by unparalleled margins. And, as for the Commissioner of MLB and team owners not to have noticed what was taking place? Aw... come on! They would have had to be naïve, if they thought the public didn't notice...*We* all did!

My thoughts

I liked an article that *Baseball Almanac* published about MLB creating a drug testing policy with some teeth in it. The undated article "suggested that at the start of the regular season every Major League player on a roster would be tested for a clearly defined set of drugs two weeks before Opening Day.

If found positive, the player would be suspended without pay for the entire season. One more positive test and the player would be banned from the game of baseball. Another test would occur the day before the All-Star Game, and a final test on the last day of the season. Same results for each of the final two tests. Players who use these drugs have done more harm to our national pastime than any group since the 1919 Black Sox.

Even today, the word *steroid,* by itself, has become an all-purpose, fear-generating rubric—similar to "terrorism" or "global warming." Clearly, any way you slice it, steroids and other PEDs are having a negative impact on baseball.

The findings related to BALCO, Biogenesis, and the Mitchell investigations have cast dark shadows on the accomplishments of many of this era's greatest superstars. And, all those statistical records that we cherished the most are now tainted. Perhaps the better title for this Steroid Era—the "Tainted Era."

I have a question: "Do you think such a suggestion as the above one by *Baseball Almanac* stands a chance of getting approved?" If you answered, "Yes," don't get your hopes up. Unfortunately, I doubt if such a common sense policy would make it to first base. We have not reached the point where everybody (MLB and Players Association) will work together to negotiate a collective bargaining agreement that will solve this problem, and rid the game of steroids and other PEDs. I think that each of the two sides believe it is in their best interest to do little more than to add a small amount of *window dressing*.

George Mitchell, in his report, made reference to "letting go of the past and looking to the future." I agree. That *Baseball Almanac* suggestion looks to the future. Mark my word, if an appropriate policy was put in place and enforced, MLB will only have to use it once and then players would be motivated to stay clean.

Afterthought

I recall reading some time back that an unknown person, both asked and answered, a single question: "Why do players take steroids?" "Because they work." True! But as a person who has spent a fair amount of time analyzing motivational factors throughout the business world, I would like to add the following three great motivators: desire to excel, desire for recognition, and desire for money—not necessarily in that order.

This entire scenario leaves me wondering about the motives of those in charge. Are they truly committed to banning all illegal PEDs from baseball? Or, is their position simply a political stance to placate the fans?

Bottom line

I don't think baseball is going to get tougher and increase the penalties for those whose steroids/PED tests are positive. Unless something dramatic takes place, the Players Association will not allow it. Instead, baseball will muddle along with a haphazard policy, hoping that fans will be distracted by those magnificent home runs and fireball pitches, and forget about the issue.

Chapter 8

The Fork
in the Road

"The farther backward you can look, the farther forward you can see."

– Winston Churchill

Now that Chapter 7 is completed, and we are fully aware that even with all of its triumph and glory, baseball's history is also riddled with mistakes, half-truths, and outright lies—the game's dark side. So, what do we now know, and what does the future hold?

Hijacking history

Well, to start off, we know that the real history of baseball was hijacked. We also know that we can forget about Abner Doubleday being the inventor of baseball, and Cooperstown being the site of the first baseball game. Oh, by the way, I was pleased to notice that the National Baseball Hall of Fame finally took a small step forward, acknowledging that a mistake was made when it credited Cooperstown as the birthplace of baseball. The Hall officially announced—in conjunction with its seventy-fifth anniversary in 2013–14: "On June 12, 1939, the National Baseball Museum opened its doors for the first time, in honor of the 100th anniversary of the mythical "first game" that allegedly was played in Cooperstown on June 12, 1839." *Oh yes, this proclamation should also mean that the story behind the "Doubleday baseball," now residing in the National Baseball Museum, is also a myth.*

With the legends of Doubleday and Cooperstown now debunked, it is time to move on to another well contrived scam that landed Alexander Joy Cartwright, Jr. in the Hall of Fame. His plaque proclaims him to be the "Father of Modern Baseball." To make matters worse, it also inaccurately credits Cartwright for three specific baseball rules: "Set bases 90 feet apart. Established 9 innings as game and 9 players as team."

Cartwright did none of these things, and every other word of substance on his plaque is false, including the notation that he "Carried baseball to Pacific Coast and Hawaii in Pioneer days." So, the Cartwright story is also a myth. *Basically, it is the same as the Doubleday myth, but with different names and places.*

According to a National Baseball Hall of Fame and Museum project at Arizona State University, "The Hall of Fame feels it is their duty to tell the truth, that they can use truth to temper some of their subject matter's inherent nostalgia, and that sticking to portrayals of the truth provides a form of moral compass for directing exhibit efforts."[i]

To tell the truth. I believe that practically every visitor who walks through the door of any reputable museum expects information to be accurate and factual. Museums do more than report facts; they argue and persuade, utilizing one very specific perspective from which to view history.

Yet, every piece of evidence that I was able to uncover strongly suggests that the National Baseball Hall of Fame is aware that the preponderance of information inscribed on the Cartwright plaque is a myth at best. But, for some unknown reason, the Hall has chosen to ignore changing those credits.

Some might offer a defense for the Hall's position, that the Cartwright plaque's inaccuracies were not uncovered until decades later. *(That, I believe to be true.)* Therefore, they might say, to expect corrections is unrealistic.

In rebuttal, I offer the following: A precedent has already been set. Roberto Clemente's original gallery plaque listed his name as "Roberto Walker Clemente," but upon performing additional research on Latino heritage, and finding out that a mother's maiden name traditionally followed a child's last name, the Hall recast Clemente's plaque to read, "Roberto Clemente Walker." *I rest my case.*

You might say it appears that the Hall has chosen the wrong "fork in the road," and has decided not to reverse their direction in the Cartwright matter; regrettable to say the least.

We have validated documentation that the truth about the rules controversy is somethat different.

William Rufus Wheaton created the Knickerbocker rules by copying a set he had drawn up in 1837, when he was playing for the Gothams Club. As for those rules credits the Hall of Fame attributes to Cartwright, the documentation indicates that these credits should be shared by two other men.

Daniel "Doc" Adams

"Doc" Adams was elected President of the New York Knickerbocker Club in 1846, and two years later, he was elected chairman of the committee charged with revising the Club's constitution and bylaws. His committee members consisted of Alexander Joy Cartwright, William Rufus Wheaton, and Louis Fenn Wadsworth.

Creditable evidence show that Adams set the base paths at ninety feet, among other notable innovations, including creating the position of shortstop—eight years after Cartwright left New York and headed west, in pursuit of the California gold rush of 1849.

Louis Fenn Wadsworth

As you may recall, in Chapter Three, player Duncan Curry spoke of a "mysterious" Mr. Wadsworth. *(See page 36.)*

As for the nine men, and nine innings—and perhaps even more— these should be credited to Louis Fenn Wadsworth. A first baseman for the Gothams and the Knickerbockers, from about 1850 to 1862, no one credited him as a contributor to the rules changes until December, 1907, when Mills took care in his final report to note a "statement made by Mr. Curry, of the pioneer Knickerbocker Club" that "a diagram, showing the ball field laid out substantially as it is today, was brought to the field one day by a Mr. Wadsworth."

Additional documents indicate that Wadsworth was the man responsible for giving the game nine innings and nine men. They reveal that just prior to the first convention of New York area ball clubs on Feb. 25, 1857, a Knickerbocker-dominated rules committee adopted Section 26, making the game seven innings, and setting the minimum number of players to a side at seven. In the convention, however, on Wadsworth's rebel motion, the assembled delegates changed the two recommendations to nine players and nine innings.

Gambling and game fixing

On Monday, May 14, 2018, the U.S. Supreme Court, by a 6–3 margin, passed down a ruling that took away Nevada's monopoly on legal sports gambling, clearing a path for states to legalize sports gambling. This ruling means that sports gambling regulations can vary greatly by individual state. Such a decision could quickly turn into a gambler's paradise, unless the U.S. Congress steps in and enacts a core regulatory framework for legalized sports betting.

Therefore, it is my opinion that Congress has now reached that critical fork in the road. They are in position to regulate sports gambling directly or, if they chose, to move in a less burdensome pathway. They can ignore their responsibility and allow each State to act on its own. For example, if left up to the discretion of individual states, we could see a brand-new world where our sports gambling options will be as plentiful as the politicians and their cronies allow.

Here's what could happen: It's not inconceivable that we could see a robot umpire calling balls and strikes; bets being placed on whether a pitch will be a strike or ball; every pitch, every swing, every moment that previously seemed meaningless, could matter; and some states may even allow bets to be placed on the exit velocity of a hit ball.

I expect to see states move quickly to enact sports betting regulations in the wake of this decision. Money is the big motivator. Estimates for the amount of money illegally wagered on sports in the U.S. annually ranges from the tens of billions to hundreds of billions. A 2017 study by the Eilers & Krejcik Gaming research firm suggested the legalization of sports gambling could generate as much as $6.03 billion in annual revenue by 2023.

Interestingly, Eilers & Krejcik Gaming does not believe that sports leagues will become directly involved in the action. Instead, the leagues would benefit from data fees, content fees, and marketing partnerships, as well as through an enhancement in consumer interest based on having more bets placed on the games. ESPN and other media entities may also benefit, as a result of consumers wanting unique content dedicated to sports betting.

Money talks, especially big money, and the financial windfall it could bring into each state. MLB Commissioner, Rob Manfred, confirmed that he is monitoring the issue and rethinking pro baseball's long held stance on the issue. "There is this buzz out there in terms of people feeling that there may be an opportunity here for additional legalized sports betting," Manfred said. "We are reexamining our stance on gambling. It's a conversation that's ongoing with the owners."

Manfred's statement sounds like Major League Baseball is now wavering on their stand of being against gambling on baseball, in order to protect the integrity of the game at all costs. Today, many sports gambling advocates argue that professional athletes are not at risk of jeopardizing the integrity of their sport, or falling prey to unscrupulous gamblers, because of their astronomical salaries. *Wrong!* Just look at the gambling-related history of such high-powered athletes as John Daily, Michael Jordan, Paul Hornung, Charles Barkley, Floyd Mayweather, and Pete Rose.

Two important facts that must not be ignored: The addictive nature of sports gambling, and the rampant risk of corruption that could threaten the integrity of athletes.

In its thirty-one page brief, the U.S. Supreme Court wrote, "The legalization of sports gambling requires an important policy choice, but the choice is not ours to make. Congress can regulate sports gambling directly, but if it elects not to do so, each State is free to act on its own. Our job is to interpret the law Congress has enacted and decide whether it is consistent with the Constitution."

"Shoeless" Joe Jackson & Pete Rose

Today, I believe it is nearly impossible to talk about gambling in baseball without bringing up "Shoeless" Joe Jackson and Pete Rose. Jackson's dishonest act, blunder, omission, or whatever you want to call his act of accepting that $5,000 payoff, established a precedent—any player who cheated or compromised the integrity of the professional game would not be considered for a place in the National Baseball Hall of Fame.

Sure, I found Joe a sympathetic character, too—especially since he was uneducated, and had to sign his name with an "X."

But, Commissioner Rob Manfred's 2015 decision denying a request to reinstate Jackson said a great deal. Manfred agreed with the rulings by Commissioner Landis, and a 1989 review of the matter by former Commissioner A. Bartlett Giamatti. He said, "I agree with that determination and conclude that it would not be appropriate for me to reopen this matter."

Next up, Pete Rose: A lot of people want to forgive him for betting on baseball. Three decades after his ban, it's easy to forget just how deeply the Cincinnati Reds' manager compromised the integrity of the game. Whatever he accomplished is now void, because he put baseball in harm's way.

Pete, you simply refused to comply with Baseball's most sacred rule:

> *"Any player, umpire, or club official or employee, who shall bet any sum whatsoever upon any baseball game in connection with which the bettor has no duty to perform shall be declared ineligible for one year. Any player, umpire, or club or league official or employee, who shall bet any sum whatsoever upon any baseball game in connection with which the bettor has a duty to perform shall be declared permanently ineligible."*

In December 2015, Baseball Commissioner Rob Manfred denied the request for Rose's reinstatement. That increases the likelihood that Rose, who currently holds the record for more base hits than any other player in history, will never reach the Hall of Fame.

In baseball's modern era, Pete Rose eclipsed the Chicago White Sox as the face of the gambling element within the game. Two years after his 1989 banishment from baseball, the Hall of Fame announced that anyone on Major League Baseball's permanently ineligible list was also ineligible for enshrinement in Cooperstown.

However, as Ted Spencer, curator of the National Baseball Hall of Fame and Museum, noted when discussing the role of the Museum, "we deal with history. This history sometimes includes drunks, bigots, criminals, and cheaters, but as long as they are a part of baseball's history, the Hall of Fame feels an obligation to include them in the narrative of baseball."

Therefore, Rose's expulsion does not stop his image from appearing in the Hall of Fame's Museum section. The exhibit area known as, "One for the Books," tracks baseball's great records and the stories behind them. The Hall acknowledges both Rose's gritty style of play, as well as his banishment for gambling, while also celebrating him as the game's all-time leader in base hits.

The exhibit proudly displays the cleats Rose wore on September 11, 1985, when he passed Ty Cobb with hit number 4,192. A photo of Rose, wearing the shoes while standing on first base immediately after the hit, accompanies the artifact.

Rose's presence in Cooperstown angers many baseball purists, who see the legacy of "Charlie Hustle" as one that tarnishes the game. Visitors view Rose's inclusion in the Museum as an endorsement of his actions. It is these visitors who misunderstand the difference between the Hall of Fame's Museum and the Plaque Gallery.

The Plaque Gallery celebrates the game's greatest players for their statistical achievements, and more recently, for the character they displayed while compiling their legendary numbers. By way of contrast, the Hall of Fame Museum tells the story of baseball—both the good and the bad.

Unfortunately, Pete Rose refused to change, so MLB Commissioner Manfred upheld his lifetime ban. Manfred wrote in his December 14, 2015 decision, "Mr. Rose's public and private comments, including his initial admission in 2004, provide me with little confidence that he has a mature understanding of his wrongful conduct, that he has accepted full responsibility for it, or that he understands the damage he has caused."

Despite the public's goodwill and support towards Rose, his transgression in refusing to comply with Major League Rule 21(d) remains as serious today as it was in 1989. This is to say, *very* serious. *Sorry Pete, I doubt if we will ever see your plaque hanging in the Hall of Fame, at least not in my lifetime.*

Doping

The use of PEDs really came to a head in the wake of the assaults on baseball's season and career home run records. In the summer of 1998, sluggers Mark McGwire and Sammy Sosa both eclipsed Roger Maris's single-season home run record set back in 1961. Three years later, San Francisco Giants' outfielder Barry Bonds did the same, and then went on to break Hank Aaron's all-time career home run record in 2007. By then, however, allegations that all three home run champions used steroids to artificially enhance their performances had become commonplace.

At the Hall of Fame, the staff's goal is to remain neutral observers in the steroid proceedings among mounting public pressure to forcefully address the issue. In a scathing article written for the *Village Voice* in 2007, author Emma Swan condemned the Hall of Fame for not taking a stand on PEDs. In part, the author expressed her frustration:

> *At a time when it's harder and harder to glorify anyone, baseball players or otherwise, and when chemistry has raced too far ahead of major league baseball for us to make any clear assessment of the last 20 years, the Hall's days as a meaningful institution—if it ever was one are dwindling. Fans seem willing to move past gambling and steroids and anything else you can throw at the game, but simply pretending that none of it ever happened is no way to maintain credibility; the Hall needs to embrace history and let the lionizing fall by the wayside. Without fully engaging in an exploration of the*

167

subject, the Hall of Fame does acknowledge the existence of steroids in a variety of fashions throughout the museum. In Today's Game, the Hall erected a panel crediting steroids, amphetamines, and other PEDs with affecting the game. It then goes on to notify visitors of the museum's intention to deal with the subject "honestly and impartially" once given "the perspective of time."

Much like with Pete Rose, some Hall of Fame visitors find the Museum's display of Bonds-related artifacts particularly repugnant. The Hall attempts to placate these visitors in its discussion of Bonds' career home runs by pointing out that "although Major League Baseball never identified Bonds as testing positive for steroids, allegations that he used performance-enhancing drugs clouded the accomplishment." But this is not enough for some fans, who deface the exhibit, using markers to put asterisks next to the artifacts celebrating Bonds' record.

For Bonds, and all the players suspected but never formally charged with using steroids, the Hall of Fame has chosen to wait and see how their story unfolds. What form the PED narrative will take, and how long it will be before it manifests itself, is something baseball fans will have to await patiently.

Final remarks

My research for this book has forced me to take a closer look at aspects of the game I've taken for granted at best, and willfully ignored at worst. My ultimate goal is see the game of baseball eliminate its darker side, and be consumed with integrity at all levels. I hope that learning the facts will help lead you to the same place.

Author's Notes

Abner Graves Letters

The following are the two letters by Abner Graves. Letter # 1 was dated April 3, 1905, and Letter # 2 was dated November 17, 1905. These copies are basically as written by Graves. The only modifications made were in the [From and To] headings.

Letter #1

[Note: All original spelling, grammatical errors, and punctuation are preserved.]

[FROM:] Abner Graves, Mining Engineer, 32 Bank Block, P.O. Box 672, Denver, Colo.

April 3rd, 1905

[TO:] Editor Beacon Journal, Akron, Ohio

Dear Sir:

I notice in saturdays "Beacon Journal" a question as to "origin of 'base ball'" from pen of A. G. Spalding, and requesting data on the subject be sent to Mr J E Sullivan, 15 Warren Street, New York.

The "American game of Base Ball" was invented by Abner Doubleday of Cooperstown, New York, either the spring prior, or following the "Log Cabin & Hard Cider" campaign of General Harrison for President, said Abner Doubleday being then a boy pupil of "Green's Select School" in Cooperstown, and the same, who as General Doubleday won honor at the Battle of Gettysburg in the "Civil War." The pupils of "Otsego Academy" and "Green's Select School" were then playing the old game of "Town Ball" in the following manner.

A "tosser" stood beside the home "goal" and tossed the ball straight upward about six feet for the batsman to strike at on its fall, he using a four inch flat board bat, and all others who wanted to play being scattered all over the near and far field to catch the ball, the lucky catcher then taking his innings at the bat while the losing batsman retired to the field. Should the batsman miss the ball on its fall and the tosser catch it on its first bounce he would take the bat and the losing batsman toss the ball.

When the batsman struck the ball into the field he would run for an out goal about fifty feet and return, and if the ball was not caught on the fly, and he could return to home goal without getting "plunked" with the ball thrown by anyone, he retained his innings same as in "old cat." There being generally from twenty to fifty boys in the field, collisions often occurred in attempt of several to catch the ball. Abner Doubleday then figured out and made a plan of improvement on town ball to limit number of players, and have equal sides, calling it "Base Ball" because it had four bases, three being where the runner could rest free of being put out by keeping his foot on the flat stone base, while next one on his side took the bat, the first runner being entitled to run whenever he chose, and if he could make home base without being hit by the ball he tallied. There was a six foot ring within which the pitcher had to stand and toss the ball to batsman by swinging his hand below his hip. There was eleven players on a side, four outfielders, three basemen, pitcher, catcher, and two infielders, the two infielders being placed respectively a little back from the pitcher and between first and second base, and second and third base and a short distance inside the base lines. The ball used had a rubber center overwound with yarn to size some larger than the present regulation ball, then covered with leather or buckskin, and having plenty of bouncing qualities, wonderful high flys often resulted. Anyone getting the ball was entitled to throw it at a runner and put him out if could hit him.

This "Base Ball" was crude compared with present day ball, but it was undoubtedly the first starter of "Base Ball" and quickly superceded "town ball" with the older boys, although we younger boys stuck to town ball and the "old cats." I well remember several of the best players of sixty years ago, such as Abner Doubleday, Elihu Phinney, John C Graves, Nels C Brewer, Joseph Chaffee, John Starkweather, John Doubleday, Tom Bingham and others who used to play on the "Otsego Academy Campus" although a favorite place was on the "Phinney farm" on west shore of Otsego lake.

"Base Ball" is undoubtedly a pure American game, and its birthplace Cooperstown, New York, and Abner Doubleday entitled to first honor of its invention.

Abner Graves

32 Bank Block, Denver, Colorado.

Letter #2

[Note: All original spelling, grammatical errors, and punctuation are preserved.]

[FROM:] Abner Graves, Mining Engineer, 32 Bank Block, P.O. Box 672, Denver, Colo.

November 17th, 1905

[TO:] A G Spaulding Esq.

170

126 Nassau Street, New York City

Dear Sir:

Your letter of 10th regarding origin of Base Ball received and contents noted. You mention sending me copy of "Spaldings Base Ball Guide for 1905," which I have not received, although I would like it to note the discussion mentioned. I am at loss how to get verification of my statements regarding the invention of base ball made in my letter of April 3rd 1905 to the "Akron, Ohio, Beacon-Journal," the carbon copy of my original draft of which I herewith enclose, this giving full particulars, and which after using, please return for my files.

You ask if I can positively name the year of Doubledays invention, and replying will say that I cannot, although am sure it was either 1839, 1840 or 1841, and in the spring of the year when we smaller boys were "playing marbles for keeps" which all stopped when ball commenced, as I remember well Abner Doubleday explaining "base ball" to the lot of us that were playing marbles in the street in front of Coopers tailor shop and drawing a diagram in the dirt with a stick by marking out a square with a punch mark in each corner for bases, a ring in center for pitcher, a punch mark just back of home base for catcher, two punch marks for infielders and four punch marks for outfielders, and we smaller boys didn't like it because it shut us out from playing, while Town Ball let in everyone who could run and catch flies, or try to catch them. Then Doubleday drew up same diagram on paper practically like diagram I will draw on back of another sheet and enclose herewith. The incident has always been associated in my mind with the "Log Cabin and Hard Cider" campaign of General Harrison, my Father being a "Militia" Captain and rabid partisan of "Old Tippecanoe."

I know it was as early as spring of 1841 because it was played at least three years before April 1844 when I started for Leyden Mass. to live that summer with my Uncle Joseph Green, the last prominent thing that I remember before starting being a big game of Base Ball on the "Phinney Farm" half a mile up the west side of Otsego Lake, between the Otsego Academy boys (Doubleday then being in the Academy), and Professor Green and his Select School boys. Great furore and fun marked opening of the game on account of the then unprecedented thing of "first man up, three strikes and out." Elihu Phinney was pitcher and Abner Doubleday catcher for Academy, while Greens had innings and Prof. Green was first at bat, and Doubleday contrary to usual practice stood close at Green's back and caught all three balls, Green having struck furiously at all with a four inch flat bat and missing all, then being hit in the back by the ball as he started to run.

While everyone laughed and roared at Green's three misses he claimed that Doubleday caught every ball from in front of the bat so there was no ball to hit, and that made the furore greater. I was an onlooker close up to catcher, and this incident so impressed me with the glories of Base Ball that on arriving at Leyden, Mass. I tried to get up a game but couldn't find anywhere near 22 boys so we had to play "Old Cat." Abner Doubleday unquestionably invented Base Ball at Cooperstown, N.Y. as an improvement on Town Ball so as to have opposing sides and limit players, and he named it Base Ball and had eleven players on each side. If any Cooperstown boys of that time are alive they will surely remember that game between the "Otsego's" and "Green's" which I surely identify as early in April 1844 before my start to Massachusetts, and I am certain it had been played at least three years earlier under same name and the larger boys had become proficient at it. Although I never saw any mention of ball playing in a newspaper when I was young, it might be that some mention of the game was made in the "Otsego Republican" about that time, said paper then (and now) being leading paper in Cooperstown.

Abner Doubleday was I think about 16 or 17 years old when he invented the game: he lived in Cooperstown but I do not know if born there. His cousin "John Doubleday" (a little younger) was born there and his father was a merchant with a store in the main four corners in Cooperstown. The Phinneys were run a large Book Bindery there, and I believe one in New York at same time. Of course it is almost impossible to get documentary proof of the invention, as there is not one chance in ten thousand that a boys drawing plan of improved ball game would have been preserved for 65 years as at that time no such interest in games existed as it does now when all items are printed and Societies and Clubs preserve everything.

All boys old enough to play Base Ball in those days would be very old now if not dead, and this reminds me of a letter. I have a letter dated April 6th 1905, from Mary, wife of "John C Graves" mentioned in my printed letter saying, "Dear Cousin, I received a paper this eve from Akron,Ohio, with an article you wrote about Base Ball! Every one of the boys you named are dead except John, and perhaps you do not know that John has been sick over a year with the gout, and now his mind is very weak so sometimes he does not know me." She was mistaken in saying all for I am aware that Nels C Brewer whom I mentioned now lives in Cleveland, Ohio, and I think his address is 230 Superior Street, or near that, and although he is aged he may possibly remember about the Base Ball. John C Graves is about 85 and still lives in Cooperstown.

Also I have a brother (Joseph C Graves) still in business in Cedar Rapids,

Iowa. I have added a few years experience since Base Ball was invented, but am still young enough to make a lively hand in a game, as I did last July, and I attribute my youth to the fact that I left Cooperstown and New York early in winter of 1848–9 for the Goldfields of California and have lived in the west ever since where the ageing climate of New York hasn't touched me. My Typewriter thinks this is a pretty long letter on one subject and I guess that is about correct, but your letter asked for as full data as possible and I have given you all the items I can in a rambling sort of way, but I think you have hea[r]d enough to pick out the gist of it and be better satisfied than if I had been less explicit or prolix. Just in my present mood I would rather have Uncle Sam declare war on England and clean her up rather than have one of her citizens beat us out of Base Ball.

Yours truly

Abner Graves, E.M.

End Notes

Chapter 1

i Foxsports.com. *Does this old-timer really belong in the Hall of Fame?* (11-21-2014)

ii www.SI.com. 6-12-1989

iii Chadwick, Henry. *Chadwick's The Game of Base Ball* (Silver Street Media 2009)

iv Richter, Francis. *Richter's History and Records of Base Ball* (McFarland & Company, 2005)

Chapter 2

i *Seneca Chief Cornplanter to President George Washington. 1790*, www.founders.archives.gov/documents

ii Pickering, James. *Cooper's Otsego Heritage: The Source of the Pioneers* (Michigan State University, 1979)

iii Cooper, William. *A Guide in the Wilderness*, pg. 13 (Dublin: Gilbert and Hedges. 1810)

iv Barzun, Jacques. *God's Country and Mine,* (Atlantic Little Brown, 1954)

v John Thorn, the official historian of Major League Baseball

vi Vlasich, James. *Legend for the Legendary: The Origin of the Baseball Hall of Fame* (Popular Press, 1990)

Chapter 3

i ESPN. "Laws of Base Ball' documents dated 1857 establish new founder of sport" (April 2016)

ii A placard in the Hall of Fame states that although later studies have called into question the accuracy of information on the plaques, the facts as engraved were believed to be accurate at the time.

iii Baseball Almanac.com: "Year in Review: 1953"

iv *New York Times.* "Myth of Baseball's Creation Endures" (November 12, 2010)

v Thorn, John. *Baseball in the Garden of Eden*, pg 296 (Simon & Schuster 2011)

vi Bakker, Pamela. *Eyes on the Sporting Scene, 1870-1930: Will and June Rankin*, pg. 131 (McFarland 2013)

vii Ibid

viii Nucciarone, Monica. *Alexander Cartwright: The Life Behind the Baseball Legend,* pg. 173 (University of Nebraska Press 2014)

ix Bakker, Pamela. *Eyes on the Sporting Scene, 1870-1930: Will and June Rankin* (McFarland 2013)

x Thorn, John. *Baseball in the Garden of Eden,* pg. 282 (Simon & Schuster 2011)

xi *Baseball Research Journal.* Volume 43, Issue 1, authors: McCue, Palmer, Hershberger, Blue, Inohiza

xii Society for American Baseball Research. Alexander Cartwright (2009)

xiii Nucciarone, Monica. *Alexander Cartwright: The Life Behind the Baseball Legend,* pg. 31 (University of Nebraska Press 2014)

xiv Bishop Museum Archives. Will of Mary Check Taylor (January 31, 1974)

xv Nucciarone, Monica. *Alexander Cartwright: The Life Behind the Baseball Legend,* pg. 187/188 (University of Nebraska Press 2014)

xvi Nucciarone, Monica. *Alexander Cartwright: The Life Behind the Baseball Legend,* pg. 183 (University of Nebraska Press 2014)

xvii ESPN. "Laws of Baseball' documents, dated 1857 establish new founder of sport" (April 8, 2016)

xviii Thorn, John. *Baseball in the Garden of Eden,* pg. 296 (Simon & Schuster 2011)

Chapter 4

i Gardner, Paul. *Nice Guys Finish Last: Sport and American Life* (Universal Books 1974)

ii *New York Times,* vol. 15, No. 4372, pg.8, col. 3 (September 29, 1865)

iii *New York Times,* vol. 15, No. 4372, pg.8, col. 3 (September 29, 1865)

iv *New York Clipper.* "How To Heave a Game" (November 11, 1865)

v Ibid

vi Ryczek, William J. *When Johnny Came Sliding Home* (McFarland & Company, Inc., 1998).

Chapter 5

i Asinof, Eliot. *Eight Men Out,* pgs. 130-1 (Holt, Rinehart and Winston, 1963)

ii Asinof, Eliot. *Eight Men Out,* pg. 5, last paragraph. (Holt, Rinehart and

Winston, 1963)

iii *Esquire*. "Inside Baseball," pg. 78 (May 1946)

iv Asinof, Eliot. *Eight Men Out*, pg. 132 (Holt, Rinehart and Winston, 1963)

v *Cleveland Plain Dealer* (October 4, 1911)

vi Asinof, Eliot. *Eight Men Out*, pgs. 58-59 (Holt, Rinehart and Winston, 1963)

vii Carney, Gene. *Burying the Black Sox*, pgs. 61-62 (Potomac Books, 2006)

viii *Sport Magazine*, John Carmichael. "The Chicago White Sox" (June 1951)

ix Ibid, pg 71

x Ibid, pg 73

xi Ibid, pg. 77

xii Ibid, pg. 95

xiii Ginsburg, Daniel. *The Fix is in: A History of Baseball Gambling and Game Fixing Scandals*, pg.123 (McFarland, 1956)

xiv Ibid, pg. 124

xv *The New Republic*. Hugh S. Fullerton, pg. 183 (October 20, 1920)

xvi *Project*. Gene Cary, "Uncovering the Fix of the 1919 World Series," Volume 13, Fall 2004, pgs. 39-49 (muse.jhu.edu)

xvii *The Sporting News*, Hugh S. Fullerton. "I Recall" (October 17, 1935)

xviii *New York Evening World*, Hugh S.Fullerton. "Is Big League Being Run for Gamblers with Players in the Deal?", pg.3 (December 15, 1919). (It is important to note that the newspaper did not run or promote the story on its front page.)

xix History.com." The Black Sox Baseball Scandal, 95 Years Ago" (October 09, 2014)

xx Keyes, Ralph. *Nice Guys Finish Seventh: False Phrases, Spurious Sayings, and Familiar Misquotations* (Harper Collins 1992)

xxi Asinof, Eliot. *Eight Men Out*, pg. 239 (Holt, Rinehart and Winston, 1963)

xxii Ibid, pg. 257

xxiii History.com. "The Black Sox Baseball Scandal, 95 Years Ago" (October 09, 2014)

xxiv Asinof, Eliot. *1919: America's Loss of Innocence*, pgs. 301-2 (Donald I. Fine, 1st edition, May 2, 1990)

xxv *The Sporting News*, Hugh Fullerton. October 17, 1935, Fullerton noted in his article, "But today, more than 15 years later, the full story never has been told and never will be, because Johnson, Comiskey, Herrmann, and Alf Austrian, the only ones who knew it all, are dead."

xxvi Gene Carney was the author of *Burying the Black Sox: How Baseball's Cover-Up of the 1919 World Series Fix Almost Succeeded* (Potomac, 2006), *Romancing the Horsehide: Baseball Poems on Players and the Game,* (McFarland, 1993), and dozens of baseball articles. He died in July 2009.

xxvii Fox News, published September 1, 2015

xxviii *The Wall Street Journal,* "Amnesty for Black Sox Third Baseman" (January 17, 1992)

Chapter 6

i https://sportsworld.nbcsports.com/set-the-record-straight

ii *New York Times,* pg. D7, "Truth is Revealed in Bets Rose Didn't Make (March 16, 2007)

iii *Washington Times* - Monday, April 16, 2007

iv *Today in Pro Football History,* April 17, 2011

v Attention Deficit Hyperactivity Disorder and Oppositional Defiant Behavior

vi Rose, Pete. *My Prison Without Bars.*(Rodale Books, 2004)

vii Dr. Timothy Fong, the Co-Director, UCLA Gambling Studies Program and Director, UCLA Addiction Psychiatry Fellowship.

viii FORBES.com: "You're Your Own Worst Enemy" (Maury Brown, Pete Rose, 12/14/2015)

ix Postal inspectors seized memorabilia from Michael Bertolini's house that contained the names of some of the most famous baseball players in history: Willie Mays, Hank Aaron, Duke Snider, Mike Schmidt and Pete Rose.

Chapter 7

i *Mitchell Report,* page SR-14: Investigation into the Illegal Use of Steroids and Other Performance Enhancing Substances by Players in Major League Baseball (December 13, 2007)

ii Canseco, Jose. *Juiced,* pg. 9 (Regan Books, 2005)

iii Canseco, Jose. *Juiced,* pg. 4 (Regan Books, 2005)

iv *Mitchell Report,* page SR-24

v *Mitchell Report,* page SR-32

vi *Mitchell Report,* page SR-33: Investigation into the Illegal Use of Steroids and Other Performance Enhancing Substances by Players in Major League Baseball (December 13, 2007)

vii Canseco, Jose. *Juiced,* pg. 281 (Regan Books, 2005)

Chapter 8

i ARIZONA STATE UNIVERSITY: Public History at the National Baseball Hall of Fame and Museum, pg. 188 (December, 2013)

About the Author

As a teenager in the early 1950s, Jack L. Hayes was the visiting team bat boy for the Washington Senators. Whenever the New York Yankees, Boston Red Sox, Detroit Tigers, Chicago White Sox, Cleveland Indians, St. Louis Browns, or Philadelphia Athletics came to play the Senators at D.C.'s Griffith Stadium; Jack was their bat boy. "It was the greatest job a kid could ever have," he says.

Jack was privy to what went on behind the scenes, in the clubhouse and the dugout, and on the field. He rubbed elbows and practiced with some of the greatest players of all time, including Mickey Mantle, Ted Williams, Satchel Paige, and other immortal stars from an era that is considered one of the greatest for America's favorite pastime.

His adult career included leading his international management consulting company and becoming a specialist on commercial crime. His three nonfiction books on global business have won several awards.

A recognized authority on the sport, Jack is a member of the Society for American Baseball Research (SABR), and an award-winning author of three nonfiction books on Major League Baseball: *Baseball's Finest Moments*; *Baseball's Archives: 1845-1959*; and *Baseball's Greatest Hits & Misses: Amazing to Zany Facts*.

Jack and his wife, Darlene, live in Central Florida.

Made in the USA
Columbia, SC
18 April 2024

34562457R00107